Language & Writing

⑧

Don Aker

Nelson Language & Writing Authors

Don Aker
David Hodgkinson
Michael Kamann, Senior Author

I(T)P Nelson

Variety! Each of the 16 units focuses on a different form of writing.

This feature previews the language skills you'll be learning.

At the end of this unit you will

Know

- the features of a historical narrative
- the functions of verbal phrases
- the functions of dashes
- how present-tense verbs can create excitement
- some exceptions to the "i before e except after c" rule

Be Able To

- write your own h[...] narrative
- differentiate infir[...] from preposition[...]

Unit **4** Historical Narrative

A brief introduction helps you get your bearings....

What is a historical narrative?

Historical narratives record information about significant events. Because these events took place in the past, the writer must research them carefully to make sure that he or she records the facts accurately. The following excerpt is from D. W. Phillips' historical narrative entitled *The Day Niagara Falls Ran Dry.*

NIAGARA FALLS

THE DAY

On the night of March 29, 1848, the unthinkable happened. The mighty Niagara Falls eased to a trickle and then fell silent for 30 puzzling hours. It was the only time in recorded history that this wonder of the world had been stilled. So incredible was the event that three decades later eyewitnesses were still being asked to sign declarations swearing that they were there when the Falls of Niagara ran dry.

Residents first realized that something was wrong when they were awakened by an overpowering, eerie silence. Inspection of the river by torches revealed only a few puddles of water in the river bed. The next morning, some 5000 sightseers from as far away as Hamilton and Buffalo jammed the roads to Niagara Falls and converged on the riverbank to see the phenomenon. The American Falls had slowed to a dribble, the British Channel was drying fast, and the thundering Canadian Horseshoe Falls were stilled.

For some, the event was an interesting curiosity. Peering down from the bank, they saw long stretches of drying mud, exposed boulders and chains of black puddles. Fish and turtles lay floundering in crevices. While thousands stood in disbelief, a few daredevils explored recesses and cavities at the bottom of the dry river gorge never before visible. They picked up bayonets, muskets, swords, gun barrels, tomahawks, and other relics of the War of 1812. Others took the historic opportunity to cross the river above and below the falls—on foot, on horseback, or by horse and buggy.

For superstitious people, [...] unusual silence and unexpl[...] phenomenon was a porten[...] divine wrath or impendin[...] As the day wore on, fear a[...] anxiety spread. Thousand[...] special church services on [...] of the border. Native peo[...] area shared in the belief [...] disaster was about to hap[...]

Tension grew until th[...] March 31, when a low [...] upstream announced th[...] the waters. Suddenly, a [...] surged down the river b[...] the falls. The deluge qu[...] the massive boulders at [...] of the falls and restore[...] present Niagara spray. [...] residents relaxed and r[...] to sleep again to the r[...] boom of the falls.

The cause of the st[...] was discovered later, [...] that had formed [...] Buffalo.... The [...]mb[...] of wind, w[...] and [...] jammed [...]dreds o[...] of to[...] of ice into [...] at th[...]eck of the la[...] [...]ntrance betw[...]

4. Arran[...] interv[...] think[...] will r[...]

5. Writ[...] wha[...] dra[...]

44

G[...]

A ve[...] mai[...]

The v[...]
Verba[...]
noun[...]

An[...]
ve[...]
no[...]

Leading off each unit—some writing to grab your attention. All the language instruction in the unit builds on the opening model.

For your convenience, we've highlighted the most important definitions and rules.

Welcome
to Nelson Language & Writing

Welcome to *Nelson Language & Writing*, specially designed to boost your language skills and improve your writing. Here is what you will find inside...

> When you see this logo, reach for your favourite pen! The best way to learn new language skills is to apply them in your own writing.

> Each unit teaches Grammar, Mechanics, Usage & Style, and Spelling skills, and includes a Writer's Workshop to guide you step by step through the writing process.

> We've included a wide variety of activities that allow you to practise new skills.

your relative. Before you begin your
~~questions~~ you have about the event that you
~~answer.~~ Concentrate on collecting details that
~~interesting.~~

~~our~~ subject to read it to check the accuracy of
~~refer~~ back to the Checkpoint, and revise your
~~ed~~ with its focus, content, and organization.

Language Link

Know
· the function of verbal phrases

Be Able To
· different~~es~~
infini~~~~
from ~~~~tional
ph~~~~

~~~~se that contains a verb form that is not the
~~~~.

~~~~bal phrases usually end in **-ing, -ed, -en,** or **-t.**
~~~~ction as adjectives, but they can also function as

~~~~n adjective modifying *they*
the bank, they saw long stretches of drying
~~~~ders and chains of black puddles.

~~~~ a noun, the subject of the verb *is*
~~~~rrier is a good way to get you~~~~

~~~~phrase is the **infinitive phra**~~~~
~~~~ *to* in front of it, and infiniti~~~~
~~~~verbs.

~~~~ a noun
on a tightrope is dangerous~~~~

~~~~ modifying *boom*
~~~~er ice jam, a boom now sits at the head~~~~

functions as an adverb modifying *climbed*
down <u>to recover articles from the War of 1812</u>.

47

Idea File
Although some writers intentionally mix both past and present verb tenses to create a particular effect, it is important not to mix tenses unnecessarily or by mistake.

1. Rewrite the following passage, correcting any inappropriate shifts in tense.

   Hurricane Hazel hit Toronto on the evening of October 15, 1954. Since hurricanes rarely if ever reach this far north, nobody was prepared for its arrival. The result was a disaster for many residents of Toronto.
   On that fateful evening, the hurricane winds are blowing at 120 km an hour. A cold front is moving in the opposite direction, and when it met the warm tropical air from the west it produced torrential rains. Low-lying areas like Holland Marsh were completely flooded, and some streets near the banks of the Humber River are submerged in a matter of minutes: some residents die and many others are left homeless as houses slip off of foundations and were carried away, with their occupants clinging desperately to the roof~~s~~

Language Link
SPELLING

Know
· some exceptions to the "**i before e except after c**" rule

You've heard the rule "**i** before **e** except after **c**." It's a helpful rule probably used it many times as you wrote words that contain **ie**. T~~~~ times, however, when this rule can't help you. What about words l~~~~ or *science*? In this mini-lesson, you will learn about some exception~~~~ "**i** before **e**" rule.

👁 Words to Watch For
All of these words contain **ei** or **ie** combinations. Some have been taken from the historical narrative at the beginning of the unit.

eerie	anxiety	scientific	brief	conscience
disbelief	relieved	yield	perceive	vein

In your notebook, make a list of 8-10 words that contain **ie** or **ei** combinations, focusing on words that are tricky to spell because they don't follow the usual pattern. You can use words from this box, the narrative, and your own reading.

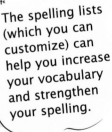

50

> You'll find plenty of tips, strategies, ideas, and challenges in these special boxes.

> The spelling lists (which you can customize) can help you increase your vocabulary and strengthen your spelling.

> You can see the goal(s) of each lesson at a glance.

I(T)P®
International Thomson Publishing

© Copyright 1998 by I(T)P® Nelson.

www.thomson.com

ISBN 0-17-606572-5

Cataloguing in Publication Data

Aker, Don, 1955-
        Nelson language and writing 8

ISBN 0-17-606572-5

1. English language - Grammar - Juvenile literature. 2. English language - Composition and exercises - Juvenile literature. I. Title.

PE1112.A38 1998   428.2   C97-931913-7

Team Leader/Publisher:	Mark Cobham
Acquisitions Editor:	Tara Steele
Project Editors:	David Friend and Jennifer Rowsell
Series Editors:	Chelsea Donaldson, Joanne Close, Karen Alliston
Art Direction:	Ken Phipps
Cover Designer:	Ken Phipps
Senior Designers:	Brian Cartwright, Daryn Dewalt, Peggy Rhodes, Todd Ryoji
Senior Composition Analyst:	Daryn Dewalt
Production Coordinator:	Theresa Thomas
Permissions:	Vicki Gould
Film:	Quadratone Graphics Ltd.

Printed and bound in Canada
2 3 4 5   02 01 00 99 98

Acknowledgments
Permission to reprint copyright material is gratefully acknowledged. Every reasonable effort to trace the copyright holders of materials appearing in this book has been made. Information that will enable the publisher to rectify any error or omission will be welcome.

"Father's Day" by permission of Joseph Mitchell. "In the Beginning" by Jackie Pearl Albany from *Tales from the Longhouse* by Indian Children of British Columbia, Gray's Publishing, 1973 & 1975. "John Henry: A Steel-Drivin' Man" from THE MAGNIFICENT MYTHS OF MAN, Eth Clifford and Leo C. Fay, The Book Society of Canada Limited, 1973. Excerpt from *Skywalking: the Life and Films of George Lucas* by Dale Pollock. Copyright © 1983 by Dale Pollock. "The Day Niagara Falls Ran Dry" reprinted with permission from *The Day Niagara Falls Ran Dry* by D. W. Phillips, 1993, Key Porter Books Ltd., Toronto. Reprinted by permission of the Publisher from The Canadian Children's Treasury by Janet Lunn, 1988, Key Porter Books Ltd., Toronto. "Canadian Rockies Sampler" reprinted by permission of Roads Less Traveled. "Alone" by Sue Kitchin from ONCE AROUND THE SUN edited by Brian Thomson. Published by Oxford University Press, Australia. Excerpt from *Obasan* copyright Joy Kogawa. Excerpt from *Who Has Seen the Wind?* by W.O. Mitchell © 1947. Reprinted by permission of Macmillan Canada. "Measure Yourself" from *How Sports Works* by the Ontario Science Centre. Used by permission of Kids Can Press Ltd., Toronto, Canada. Text copyright © 1988 by The Centennial Centre of Science and Technology. "Earthride" from SIERRA CLUB BOOK ON WEATHER WISDOM by Vicki McVey. Copyright © 1991 Vicki McVey. By permission of Little, Brown and Company. "Welcome to ESP" adapted from "Scary Science" by Sylvia Funston with permission of the Publisher, © 1996 Greey de Pencier Books, Inc., Toronto, Canada. "Human Error Creates 'Serious Trouble'" printed with permission of The Associated Press. "This Bat Doesn't Fly" reprinted with permission from the Ottawa Citizen. "Ads in Our Schools" reprinted by permission of The Toronto Star.

Reviewers
The authors and publishers gratefully acknowledge the contributions of the following educators:

Carol Anastasi
Mississauga, Ontario

David Bergen
Winnipeg, Manitoba

Steve Britton
Winnipeg, Manitoba

Christopher Carroll
Langley, British Columbia

Arlene Christie
Calgary, Alberta

Dena Domijan
Burnaby, British Columbia

Genevieve Dowson
Hamilton, Ontario

Karen Gatto
Kitchener, Ontario

Irene Heffel
Edmonton, Alberta

Pat Lychak
Edmonton, Alberta

Sharon Morris
Toronto, Ontario

Louis Quildon
Hamilton, Ontario

Sandra Roy
Kitchener, Ontario

Rick Smith
Odessa, Ontario

Steven Van Zoost
Windsor, Nova Scotia

Contents

7

Language Strands

(Mini-Lessons by Category)

Language Strands

The Writing Process

You're probably familiar with the stages of the writing process: prewriting, drafting, revising, editing and proofreading, and presenting. You probably also know how *messy* the writing process can be. You might find yourself reorganizing your information as you write. Or you might be well into the revising stage when you suddenly realize that you have to go back and think again about your purpose in writing. That's why we've put in all the two-way arrows in the diagram (and why our little writer person spends a lot of time darting back and forth between stages).

In the first stage, **prewriting**, you choose a topic, define your purpose and audience, and organize your ideas. Notice the arrows that point to and away from this stage. Prewriting connects to all the other stages because the questions you ask yourself at the outset about audience and purpose really determine how you will write, revise, *and* edit your work.

So now you've transformed the whirling thoughts in your head into a structured list of the things you want to write about. If you're like our little writer person, you're excited: you've progressed to the **drafting** stage. As you write, you'll need to remember your purpose, your audience, and your plan of organization. Think about how to capture your audience's attention (and how to keep it)—but try not to worry much about what your writing sounds like, or about details of grammar, spelling, usage, or punctuation. This is the time to let it *flow!*

When you're **revising** your draft, you need to consider three things: focus, content, and organization. Have you done what you set out to do? Is your writing style geared to the people you want to reach? Is there anything that you've missed, that you want to expand on, move somewhere else, or cut altogether? Now is the time to decide. Be brave, be ruthless, listen to your inner voice—and make those changes! Then go make yourself some hot chocolate.

By the time you're ready for **editing and proofreading**, you should be more or less satisfied that you've achieved your purpose in writing. This stage is a time for tinkering with words, and for tidying up mistakes in grammar, spelling, usage, and punctuation. (The units in this book will give you lots of ideas about what to look for when you're editing.) Finally, when you're **presenting** your work, make sure that it looks sharp: that it's clearly laid out, and nicely bound together. In other words, give your presentation some polish!

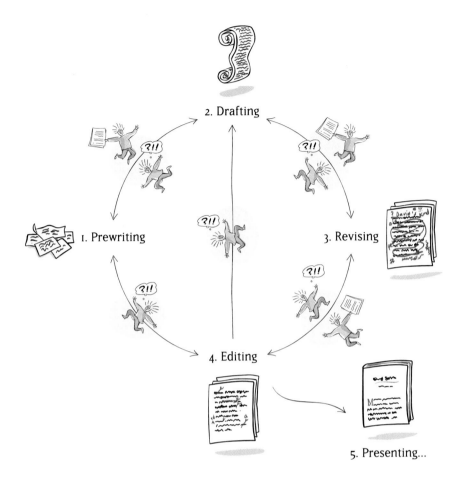

2. Drafting

1. Prewriting

3. Revising

4. Editing

5. Presenting...

Tony Gets an Assignment
(or, The Web and Flow of a Writer's Life)

Tony has been given a writing assignment:

> *Write a biographical incident that reveals something about the personality of someone you know.*

Tony is stumped. Blocked. In short, he can't think of a *thing*.

1. PREWRITING

No, we're not talking about going out and buying pens. This is the stage where you think about what you want to write about, and whether it will work as a topic. (For example, you might *want* to write a biographical incident that reveals the personality of Binky your goldfish, but this might not work if Binky doesn't *have* a personality.)

Tony figured that the best way to begin was to make a list of everyone he knew. Just looking at the list helped him to think of a few incidents, and here's the web he made of those events:

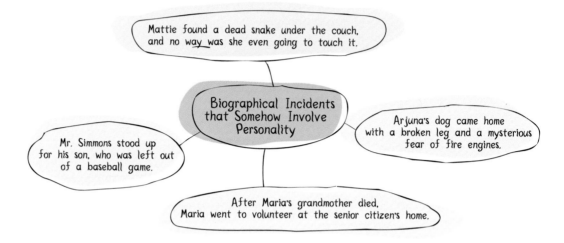

Choosing a Topic

When **choosing a topic**, ask yourself

What do I find interesting about this topic?
Do I know enough about this topic to write about it?
Does this topic meet the assignment requirements?

Tony considered these four incidents, and finally decided to write about Mr. Simmons. What Mr. Simmons did had really impressed Tony. He remembered it well; it wouldn't take too much time to describe; and above all, it revealed a strength of character about Mr. Simmons that Tony hadn't seen before.

Defining a Purpose and Audience

When **defining your purpose and audience**, ask yourself

Why am I writing this?
Who am I writing for?

Your answers will affect everything, from what you say to how you say it, so it's worth doing a little thinking beforehand to save yourself time and effort later.

After asking the question "Why am I writing this?" Tony couldn't help himself: "I'm writing this because I have to!"

But Tony has chosen to tell this *particular* story because he has very clear memories of Mr. Simmons, who was Tony's grade two teacher. Because of an illness, Mr. Simmons had a patch over one eye and walked with a cane. Everyone thought he was a good teacher, but one day Tony was inspired by something that Mr. Simmons did outside of the classroom. And now Tony would like to capture that moment. His audience? Well, his teacher, obviously. And the other kids in the class (some of whom remember Mr. Simmons from elementary school).

Organizing Ideas

When **organizing ideas**, ask yourself

> Does the type of writing suggest a possible order?
> What order will make my ideas most interesting/understandable/appealing to my audience?
> What key words will help me order my ideas?

Tony has generated a list of details he wants to include. Because he's writing a narrative, he's decided that chronological order makes the most sense. Here's his outline:

- spring excitement
- baseball season
- Douglas Simmons wants to play baseball with the boys
- he's clumsy—lack of practice, so not as good as the other boys
- Mr. Simmons gives Douglas baseball glove hoping he'll be able to play with other kids
- watches as Douglas tries to join a ball game on playground
- Douglas feels rejected
- Mr. Simmons feels bad, both for son and for himself
- realizes his illness has affected more than just himself— his son too

2. DRAFTING

When **drafting**, ask yourself

> What's my purpose and who is my audience?
> How will I get and keep my audience's attention?
> What key words or phrases can I use to keep my writing logical and easy to follow?

The Writing Process

Outline in hand, Tony got out his lucky pen and set to work. Well, actually, he stared at the page for some time, pen poised to begin.

If you're finding it hard to get the words down, try

- setting a timer for ten minutes and writing nonstop about anything
- recopying what you've already written
- explaining to a friend or classmate what you're trying to say
- refocusing on your purpose and your audience

Tony knew he needed a great beginning: *On that fateful day, so long ago, the sun was shining, the birds were singing....* Oh man, this was harder than he thought.

To get your audience's attention, try

- starting with a question that will make them think
- using dialogue
- quoting an expert
- presenting an interesting fact

Tony finally began his draft with a description of Mr. Simmons looking out the school window at the boys playing baseball, the details of his illness, and how it had prevented him from playing baseball with his son. Tony strayed a bit from his outline because he realized that all this information was important for the point of the story.

But after a couple of pages Tony got worried because he hadn't even *started* writing about the actual incident. (And the whole thing was supposed to be only a few paragraphs!) So he crammed the rest of the story into one more paragraph. Tony, now hunched over his desk and writing furiously, ended with a fluorish: *"How is my son supposed to learn how to play if you don't let him?" cried the heartbroken Mr. Simmons to the boys, and tears were brimming in his one eye.*

There. Done! Tony leaned back in his chair, thinking his private thoughts. (They sounded something like this: "Yep, yep, yep. Am I good or *what?*")

3. REVISING

When **revising**, ask yourself

Are my purpose and audience clear?
What do I like best about my writing?
Does every part of the writing relate to my purpose?
Is there anything missing?

?

Revision can be the most difficult part of the writing process. We're so close to our own writing that it's hard to be objective about it. So, if possible, don't revise your work right away. Let it sit overnight or longer, so that you can gain some perspective on it. That's what Tony did. When he read his amazing creation a couple of days later—well, he wrinkled his brow. Narrowed his eyes. Pursed his lips. Hmm. Perhaps it needed a *little* work....

When you revise your draft, try to look at the big picture before you tackle the details. Concentrate on three things: focus, content, and organization.

Focus

Writing is focused if

- it's structured to emphasize the main point
- it achieves the purpose you set out to achieve
- it's directed at the audience you set out to write for

Content

When checking the content of your writing, make sure

- everything you say helps you to achieve your purpose
- you've included enough information for your audience
- you haven't included any unnecessary information

Organization

When revising the order of your writing, decide if

- the information is arranged to suit your purpose and audience
- any paragraphs or sentences should be added, deleted, or rearranged to make your point more effectively

When Tony really considered his draft he realized that he'd have to make some changes. He needed to shorten the introductory part about Mr. Simmons (too much description at the beginning sort of slowed things down, and maybe all the details about his illness weren't so important after all). He'd also need to make the incident itself more dramatic (shorter sentences, more dialogue), and end on a more positive note. Tony saw that his last sentence made Mr. Simmons sound kind of pathetic, and actually the *point* of the story was the exact *opposite.*

Sigh.

The Writing Process

4. EDITING AND PROOFREADING

When **editing and proofreading**, ask yourself

Have I used as few words as possible to achieve my purpose?
Are my words well chosen, given my audience and purpose?
Are my sentences clear?
What particular grammar, mechanics, usage, and spelling errors
should I check for?

At last Tony had a draft that he was happy with—or at least, that said what he wanted it to say. Now it was time to polish his writing.

But it can be difficult to edit your work if you don't know what to look for. The units in this book contain mini-lessons that will help you to focus on a few points in each piece of writing you do. That way, as you become aware of the mistakes you tend to make, you can gradually compile your own list of what to watch for when you edit.
of what to watch for when you edit.

- Look for ways to make your writing sound better (word choice, sentence variety, etc.).
- Correct grammatical, mechanical, and spelling errors (compile your own checklist of things to watch for).
- Say what you want to say using as few words as possible. Be ruthless.
- Keep a personal dictionary of words you frequently misspell.
- Get someone else to help you proofread your work.

Now, Tony happens to be a little weak in the spelling department, but fortunately he knows it. For help he turned to his friends Chris and Mattie. They found several spelling mistakes, and also discovered (annoyingly) that Tony has a tendency to write run-on sentences.

Here's the final draft of Tony's biographical incident.

The snow had melted and it was the time of year for baseball.
Gerald Simmons had loved playing ball as a kid. Now, a cane and
the patch over his left eye forced him to watch the students
from the window of his classroom. That morning, he had given
his son his old baseball glove, hoping that Douglas would enjoy
the sport as much as he had.

Douglas gulped the last bite of his lunch and rushed out with his dad's old-fashioned glove. He stumbled out to the field, to find the teams already picked and the first pitches thrown. "What team am I on?" Douglas called enthusiastically. "What team do I play for?" he repeated the question uneasily. There was no response.

From his window, Mr. Simmons watched Douglas retreat, dangling the unused glove. Angrily, he reached for his cane and headed out to the baseball diamond. He ached as he remembered that he had never been able to practise with Douglas because of his health. "How is my son supposed to learn how to play if you don't let him?" he cried.

But he was a teacher as well as a father, and acceptance was a lesson he could help these children to learn. With a shrug, he regained his composure. "I haven't been able to help him," he said simply. "He needs a chance and I'm asking you to give it to him." And with that Mr. Simmons turned and walked slowly away.

Way to go, Tony! Look at his first paragraph: in just four sentences he sets the scene, introduces Mr. Simmons, and leads into Douglas's dilemma. Notice how his sentences flow, and how each paragraph has a central focus and moves the story forward. This helps to keep his readers interested. Tony has even used some vivid verbs that help the reader visualize the action. And Tony has organized his whole story around that one final character-revealing moment (which, as you'll recall, was the whole purpose of the piece).

Good writing seems effortless when you read it, but it can take a lot of thinking, rewriting, revising, and correcting before it reaches its final form. (Ask Tony.) The rest of this book can help you cultivate the skills you'll need to develop, shape, and polish your writing. Now get out your lucky pen.

Narration

Narration, the telling of a story, is as much a part of our culture as the food we eat or the clothing we wear. Although many people think of novels and short stories as the most common forms of narration, there are stories everywhere around us. Letters we write and receive, cafeteria chatter, and even our telephone conversations are filled with narratives, because when people share an experience with others, they often do so by telling a story.

This section contains four forms of narrative writing: myth, legend, biography, and historical narration. Although they contain varying degrees of fact and fiction, they all tell stories that entertain and inform us.

Features of Narration

- A narrative is a story developed from an event or series of events.

- Narration usually involves a character in some kind of conflict.

- Character, setting, and mood are usually established at the beginning of the story. The middle of the story describes events in which the character deals with the main conflict, and the end of the story tells how the conflict is resolved.

- Narrative writers often keep their readers interested by including details, such as description and dialogue, that show rather than tell what happened.

Unit 1 Myth

What is a myth?

Myths are stories passed down from generation to generation within a culture. Myths often explain the natural world in a supernatural way. The following myth is called "In the Beginning," by Jackie Pearl Albany (told to her by her mother).

Long, long ago when the world was very young, Nanabozo, the creator, as the Indians believed, found himself very much alone. There was nothing but water and air everywhere. He became very lonely. So as not to be alone he created the muskrat, beaver, and otter, but soon they grew tiresome as companions.

He wondered why he grew tired of their company. He decided he needed different creatures as companions. But there was too much water.

"The water is not solid enough," he said to himself. "I need something on which to rest my feet. I think that if I could stand on something solid, I could put one foot in front of the other and walk around."

After further thought, he tied his longest fishing line to the muskrat, and told him to dive as deep as he could and try to bring something up from the bottom of the water. The muskrat was gone a long, long, time, and when he finally came up he was so tired that he died. But Muskrat did not fail, because between his tiny paws was a little ball of mud.

Know

- the characteristics of myths
- the four most important parts of speech
- most of the rules for using commas
- what a root word is and how related words are made

Be Able To

- tell and write a myth
- identify the function of a word in the context of a sentence
- improve your writing by using strong verbs

Nanabozo took this little piece of mud and rolled it, and rolled it, and shaped it until it grew larger, and larger, and larger. When he was through rolling and kneading and moulding, the ball of mud was so large that thousands and thousands of creatures could live with Nanabozo as companions. Plants could grow and rivers could flow.

Being in such a hurry to create, Nanabozo left wet stretches here and there which will never be dry. These lands we know as muskeg.

Nanabozo could now rest happily and proudly because of his handiwork. He had more companions and he could put one foot in front of the other and move about the beautiful world which he had built.

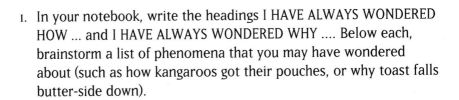

WRITER'S WORKSHOP

Language Link

Checkpoint: Myth

Discuss how these general characteristics of a myth apply to the model. Later, you can use the list to help you revise your own work.

- ✓ It usually explains an aspect of the world or expresses a cultural belief.
- ✓ It sometimes involves supernatural powers.
- ✓ It is usually written in chronological (time) sequence.
- ✓ The setting is usually the distant, mythological past.
- ✓ It often contains repeated words to make it easier for a storyteller to remember.

1. In your notebook, write the headings I HAVE ALWAYS WONDERED HOW ... and I HAVE ALWAYS WONDERED WHY .... Below each, brainstorm a list of phenomena that you may have wondered about (such as how kangaroos got their pouches, or why toast falls butter-side down).

2. Invent a supernatural being who is responsible for one of these phenomena. Give your being a name, and jot down a brief explanation of who or what this being is and a brief account of what he, she, or it did.

3. Myths usually begin as stories that are told out loud. Practise telling your myth to several different partners. Ask each of your listeners if there are any details you need to add or change to improve your story. Every time you retell it, try to incorporate the changes you think are worthwhile. Then write a draft based on the spoken (oral) version of your myth.

4. Refer back to the Checkpoint, and revise your work until you are satisfied with its focus, content, and organization.

22

GRAMMAR

A word is just a word until it is used in a sentence. Then it takes on the role of one of the eight **parts of speech**. The four most important parts of speech are **nouns, verbs, adjectives,** and **adverbs.**

A **noun** is a word that names a person, place, thing, idea, or quality.

Person	Place	Thing	Idea or Quality
Nanabozo	world	mud	creator
		muskrat	nothing
		handiwork	

Nouns that name specific people, places, or things and are capitalized are called **proper nouns**. *Nanabozo* and *Muskrat* are proper nouns in the model.

A **verb** is a word that shows an action or state of being.

He **tied** his longest fishing line to the muskrat.

Sometimes a verb may be made up of more than one word: a **main verb** and a **helping verb**.

helping main
verb   verb
He <u>could</u> <u>put</u> one foot in front of the other.

An **adjective** is a *modifier*, a word that gives information about another word. An adjective describes or tells about a noun or pronoun.

Between his **tiny** paws was a **little** ball of mud.

Tiny modifies *paws; little* describes *ball.*

An **adverb** is a modifier that describes a verb, an adjective, or another adverb.

Nanabozo could **now** rest **happily** and **proudly** because of his handiwork.

Now, happily, and *proudly* all modify the verb *rest.*

A word can function as different parts of speech, depending on how it is used in a sentence.

For example, the word *mud* functions as an adjective in *mud puddle,* and as a noun in the sentence *He rolled in the mud.*

1. Identify the part of speech of each of the words in boldface. Then write another sentence using the same word as a different part of speech.

   a) Plants could grow and rivers could **flow**.
   b) The muskrat was gone a long, long **time**.
   c) Nanabozo shaped it until it grew **larger**.
   d) Nanabozo left wet **stretches** here and there which will never be dry.

2. Nouns, verbs, adjectives, and adverbs are the most important parts of speech because we can use them to write complete sentences. Identify which part of speech each word functions as in the following sentences.

   a) Other cultures have somewhat different mythic heroes.
   b) The Micmac had a giant, Glooscap.
   c) Glooscap supposedly formed the Annapolis Valley, barehanded!

3. Make up four more complete sentences that each contain only these four parts of speech. Above each word, identify its function.

A Challenge

Look for nouns, verbs, adjectives, and adverbs in the first paragraph of the Nanabozo myth. How many of these can you find?

MECHANICS

Writers use commas more than any other form of punctuation. In the first four sentences of the myth, for example, there are eight commas. Here are some of the most important uses for a comma.

Know
- most of the rules for using commas

Use	Example
Between each item in a series.	*Nanabozo is strong, gentle, and sometimes mischievous.*
To replace the word *and* between two or more adjectives.	*Native storytellers tell interesting, humorous stories about this mythic hero.*
After an introductory group of several words.	*When Nanabozo created the dry land, the world filled up with animals and plants.*
To set off words that interrupt a flow of thought.	*Muskrat, I'm afraid, died in his attempt to get the ball of mud.*
To separate two complete sentences joined together by the words *and, but, or, nor, so,* or *yet.*	*He created the dry land, but he left some wet patches.*
To separate words or expressions that refer to the same person or thing.	*Nanabozo's friend, Muskrat, dived to the bottom.*

For more on compound sentences, see Unit 14.

1. Explain the use of each of the commas in the first paragraph of the myth using one of the above rules.

2. Try writing your own (mythic!) paragraph, incorporating as many of these rules for commas as you can. Copy your paragraph without the commas, and challenge a partner to add commas where they are needed.

For how to use commas in quotations, see Unit 3.

3. Write another rule to explain the use of the comma in the following direct quotation from the model. Compare your rule with that of one or two of your classmates.

   "The water is not solid enough," he said to himself.

Unit **1** Myth

USAGE & STYLE

Know

- improve your writing by using strong verbs

Verbs are among the strongest tools a writer can use. The more specific and vivid they are, the more compelling your writing will be.

Acceptable: Nanabozo **worked** the mud in his hands.

Better: Nanabozo **rolled, kneaded,** and **moulded** the mud in his hands.

1. In your notebook, identify which verb in each of the following pairs is more effective, and explain why.

   a) The mud **moved** between Nanabozo's fingers.
   The mud **oozed** between Nanabozo's fingers.
   b) Pieces of mud **plopped** into the water.
   Pieces of mud **fell** into the water.
   c) The muskrat **sliced** through the water.
   The muskrat **swam** through the water.
   d) Nanabozo **bit** the apple.
   Nanabozo **crunched** the apple.

2. Write a specific verb that could take the place of each of the following phrases (you may want to consult a thesaurus).

   a) walked happily   b) walked angrily   c) walked fearfully
   d) walked quietly   e) walked loudly   f) walked quickly

3. Identify all the verbs you have used in your myth. Circle any that do not create strong sensory images, and try to replace them with specific verbs that convey vivid impressions of your subject.

SPELLING

Know

- what a root word is and how related words are made

A root word, or base word, is a word or word part to which prefixes and suffixes are added to make new words. When a suffix is added, one or more letters may be dropped from the root word.

honest   honesty, dishonest, honestly
relate   related, relating, relationship

Words to Watch For

All of these words contain a root to which a suffix has been added. Some have been taken from the myth at the beginning of the unit. The others are words you might use when writing about myths. For more on suffixes, see Unit 5.

creator	believed	natural	historical	civilization
companions	explanation	appreciation	cultural	scarcity

In your notebook, make a list of 8-10 words that contain a root word and a prefix and/or a suffix. You can use words from this box, the myth, and your personal reading. Write the root beside each word.

1. Many words we use today are derived from Latin and Greek roots. For example, the Latin word for citizen—**civis**—forms the root of words like *city, civic, civil, civilian,* and *civilization.* Make a class chart of Latin and Greek roots and their related words. (Hint: A dictionary that contains etymologies will help you do this task.)

 Strategy

A **Personal Dictionary** is a list of words you have difficulty spelling. Beside each word, write a sentence that includes the word in order to illustrate what it means. Keep your Personal Dictionary handy when you are proofreading so that you can use it and add to it easily.

2. Change each word to the form indicated in brackets by modifying its suffix. Write the new words in your notebook.

   a) explanation (verb)   b) appreciation (adjective)   c) historical (noun)
   d) scarcity (adjective)   e) natural (adverb)   f) creator (verb)

Scroll Back

Edit and proofread your myth, paying particular attention to the following checklist:

❏ Have you used commas correctly?
❏ Have you used strong verbs whenever possible?
❏ Are all words spelled correctly, especially those that contain prefixes and suffixes?

Unit **1** Myth

Unit ② Legend

What is a legend?

Legends are stories that are often based on some kernel of truth. The hero or heroine may have been a real person, or the event in the legend really may have happened. But as legends are passed down, storytellers exaggerate aspects of the story, so they often end up to be more fiction than fact. Here is the legend of "John Henry: A Steel-Drivin' Man."

The word went out quickly.

It spread from hill to hill and from valley to valley. John Henry, the man who could outwork ten men, would go up against a machine. John Henry, known to all as the strongest man in the South, would drive steel against a steamhammer.

All through the night people moved toward the mountains. Some were John Henry's friends, and some were his relatives. Some were strangers who had only heard tell of the tall black man whose strength equalled ten. One and all, they wanted to see John Henry drive steel against a machine, and, one and all, they wanted to see John Henry win.

John Henry's folks came, and his wife, Sally Ann, came too. John Henry's ma cried and grabbed John Henry by the hand. "Don't do it, John Henry," she begged. "Don't race that machine. Don't you remember what you told me once when you were just a little tyke? You picked up your daddy's hammer and you said, 'I'm gonna die with a hammer in my hand.' Don't you remember that, John Henry?"

"I remember," John Henry answered. "But I'm a natural man, a steel-drivin' man, and I got to beat that machine or die trying."

The machine started fast and drove steel well into the mountains. But John Henry started faster still and drove steel deeper than anyone had ever seen. He had a forty-pound hammer in each hand, and he held the spikes between his teeth like pins. Running, he spat the spikes into the mountainsides and drove them home with flying hammers that looked like rainbows sitting on his shoulders.

Know

- the characteristics of a legend
- the functions of prepositions, pronouns, conjunctions, and interjections
- how hyphens are used
- what onomatopoeia is
- some common three-consonant patterns and the sounds they make

Be Able To

- create your own legendary comic book hero
- divide words properly at the end of a line
- create onomatopoeic words

At noon, John Henry and the steamhammer were tied dead even. When the sun passed its zenith and headed down the other side of the sky, John Henry pulled ahead. Then the machine pulled even and went in front. John Henry groaned, and his hammers sounded like great church bells. Soon John Henry came even with the machine. And the pounding of his heart drowned out the rat-a-tat-tat of the steamhammer.

The day grew late and the sun touched the tops of the peaks. John Henry and the machine were still dead even. John Henry's pounding heart shook the mountains so that the people feared for their lives.

"He'll never make it," the people cried. "John Henry'll never beat that machine. He done his best, but no man can outlast a machine."

Now the sun was nearly gone. Only one red point glowed over the tallest peak. The machine was one spike ahead.

"I'm gonna beat that machine," John Henry cried. "I'm gonna beat that machine or die trying."

John Henry's hammers flashed and rang like bells from heaven. He caught up. He went ahead by one spike, then by two, then three. The tiny point of sun disappeared, and the race was over. John Henry had won. The crowd began to cheer.

Suddenly John Henry's chest heaved and his thundering heart drove him to the ground, his hammers in his hands. The people gasped.

And then a great silence fell on the mountains. The steamhammer had ceased its rat-a-tat-tat. John Henry's hammers no longer rang out. And John Henry's pounding heart no longer echoed among the peaks like drums.

So they buried John Henry in the mountains. They buried him with his hammers in his hands. To this day, they still tell about the race between John Henry and the steamhammer. And trains pass by these words carved in the rocks: HERE LIES A STEEL-DRIVIN' MAN.

WRITER'S WORKSHOP

Checkpoint: Legend

Discuss how these general characteristics of a legend apply to the model. Later, you can use the list to help you revise your own work.

✓ It often contains language that creates strong sensory impressions.

✓ It usually involves a hero who performs amazing feats.

✓ It tends to exaggerate.

1. Working with a partner, list three or four figures whom you consider heroes in each of the following categories: SPORTS, POLITICS, ENTERTAINMENT, and FICTION. Beside each person, identify what qualities he or she possesses that appeal to you.

2. Now, choose one of these figures and transform him or her into a comic book superhero! How can you embody the good qualities you associate with the person in the way your superhero looks, sounds, and acts? How will his or her personal history reflect these qualities?

3. Think of a real or imagined incident that shows your hero at his or her best. Use this incident as the basis for writing the first episode in the adventures of your hero. If you are using a real incident, remember to exaggerate!

4. Revise and rewrite your episode until you are satisfied with its focus, content, and organization.

GRAMMAR

Know

- the functions of prepositions, pronouns, conjunctions, and interjections

Nouns, verbs, adjectives, and adverbs are the four basic parts of speech because we can write complete sentences using them. However, there are four other parts of speech: **pronouns, prepositions, conjunctions,** and **interjections.**

> A **pronoun** is a word that takes the place of a noun.

The word went out quickly. **It** spread from hill to hill....

It replaces *the word*.

Other pronouns include words like *I, me, you, we, ours, they, theirs, us, some,* and *everybody*.

> A **preposition** is a word that shows the relationship between a noun or pronoun and another word in the same sentence.

John Henry was the strongest man **in** the South.

The word *in* is a preposition because it shows a relationship between *man* and *South*. Other prepositions include *across, along, at, before, between, by, from, in, through, under,* and *with*.

> A **conjunction** is a joining word that connects words or groups of words.

There are two kinds of joining words. **Coordinating conjunctions** join the same kinds of structures, such as two (or more) nouns, verbs, or sentences. The four most common coordinating conjunctions are *and, but, nor,* and *or*.

Then the machine pulled even **and** went in front.

Subordinating conjunctions join only sentences, and one of these sentences depends on the other.

subordinating conjunction

John Henry's hammers flashed, <u>until</u> he caught up.

The word *until* joins two sentences by turning the second sentence *(He caught up)* into a clause *(until he caught up)*. This clause now depends on the first sentence *(John Henry's hammers flashed)* for its meaning. Other subordinating conjunctions are *although, as, because, before, since, unless, until,* and *while*.

For more on clauses, see Unit 9.

> An **interjection** is a word or group of words that shows strong feeling or sudden emotion.

Well, John Henry was a steel-drivin' man.

Man! He sure taught that machine a thing or two!

Unit **2** Legend

1. Identify whether the words in boldface are pronouns, prepositions, conjunctions, or interjections.

   a) John Henry was an American folk hero, **and** all the people loved **him**.
   b) In Canada, **we** have created a legendary figure out **of** Joe Montferrand.
   c) **He** was just a lumberjack, **eh**, but his strength was well known **throughout** the Ottawa Valley.
   d) Many Canadians were introduced **to** Joe Montferrand's supposed exploits **when** Stompin' Tom Connors wrote a song called "Big Joe Mufferaw."

2. Working with a partner or on your own, list all the pronouns, prepositions, and conjunctions in the sixth paragraph (beginning *At noon ...*) of the model.

3. Some words can act as either prepositions or subordinating conjunctions. Identify the part of speech of each word in boldface.

   a) John Henry put his pride **before** his life.
   b) He finished hammering **before** the machine did.
   c) **Since** you enjoyed this legend, you should try writing one yourself.
   d) I haven't read a comic book **since** Tuesday.

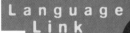

MECHANICS

Know
- how hyphens are used

Be Able To
- divide words properly at the end of a line

Use a hyphen when necessary to link two parts of a **compound modifier**.

I'm a natural man, a **steel-drivin'** man....

1. Look at the use of the hyphen in the example above. Why do you think it is necessary? (Hint: What word does *steel* modify?) Based on this example, write a brief explanation of what a compound modifier is.

2. Explain the shift in meaning between the following pairs of words by drawing pictures in your notebook to illustrate each descriptive phrase:

a) two-footed creatures	two footed creatures
b) blue-uniformed students	blue, uniformed students
c) far-flung friends	far, flung friends

A Challenge

Taking out the hyphen in a compound modifer can turn a descriptive phrase into an absurd or funny expression. Try to come up with a few of your own descriptive phrases that have a rather different meaning without the hyphen in the compound modifier. List the two versions of each phrase side by side for contrast.

3. Now look at the following expressions and explain why they do NOT need a hyphen.

   carefully made quilt   dangerously close call   badly conceived plan

4. Based on the information you have gathered about hyphens, try writing a rule that will help you and your classmates remember when to hyphenate compound modifiers.

Hyphens are also used to **divide a word** of two or more syllables at the end of a line.

Whenever possible, avoid dividing words. When you do divide, be sure to do so between syllables. Never divide a proper noun.

5. Correct any badly divided words below by rewriting the line endings in your notebook. (Check a dictionary for syllable breaks.)

> All through the night people moved toward the mount-
> ains. Some were John Henry's friends, and some we-
> re his relatives. Some were strangers who had only
> heard tell of the tall black man whose strength equal-
> led ten. One and all, they wanted to see John Hen-
> ry drive steel against a machine, and, one and all,
> they wanted to see John Henry win.

Unit **2** **Legend**

Hyphens are used between **compound numbers** written as words, from 21 to 99 (for example, *forty-five*). Hyphens are also used in **fractions** written as words (for example, *two-thirds*).

6. Check through three pieces of your own writing, and correct any errors you made in the use of hyphens.

Techno Tip

If you set your word-processing program to divide words automatically at the end of the line, be sure to do a global search for hyphens (-) and check that the word divisions are correct. Also, avoid editing your document after you have inserted hyphens, or you may end up with words hyphenated in the middle of a line.

Language
Link

USAGE & STYLE

Know
- what onomatopoeic is

An **onomatopoeic** word imitates the sound that is associated with its meaning.

Be Able To
- create onomatopoeic words

Onomatopoeia can make your writing more vivid by appealing to your readers' sense of hearing. Here are some examples of onomatopoeic words:

crack   gurgle   snap   crash   murmur

1. Find three examples of onomatopoeia in the legend of John Henry. Hint: Saying a word aloud will help you to compare its sound to its meaning. For example, the word *spat* ("he *spat* the spikes") sounds like what it means.

2. Invented words are often the best way to capture sounds in writing. For example, when describing the sounds of a hot summer day, one student wrote that he heard "the *zzzrrreeeEEEEEE* of a locust." Choose a location you are familiar with (for example, a school hallway, a swimming pool, a fast-food restaurant, a lake) and invent at least one word that imitates a sound that would be heard there.

3. Make a list of onomatopoeic words *(wham! biff!)* that you associate with comic books. Consider whether you can use any of them in your superhero episode.

SPELLING

In some three-consonant patterns, each consonant can be heard. For example, you can hear the three consonants **s, p,** and **r** in *spring*. These patterns are called **blends**. Other three-consonant patterns make two sounds, not three. In the word *shrine*, for example, the **sh** pattern is a digraph (two consonants that combine to make one sound). The consonant **r** adds the second sound.

Words to Watch For

All of these words contain a three-consonant pattern. Some words are from the legend. The others are words you might use when you write your comic.

spread	strangers	structure	transcribe	triumph
strongest	strength	threatened	thrilled	wretched

In your notebook, make a list of 8-10 words that begin with a three-consonant pattern. You can use words from this box or your personal reading.

1. Find the word in the box that has two three-consonant patterns. Write the word, circling the pattern that contains a digraph.

2. In your notebook, write the word from the box that completes each of these sentences.
   a) The horse's _____ and speed were unequalled.
   b) Stories of her amazing powers _____ across the land.
   c) The people were _____ because their hero had fallen.
   d) He fought to _____ over the mighty machine.

3. Choose five words from your list that you can use to create a description of your hero. Write the description, capturing the essence of your hero in a few sentences. Add an illustration, and you'll have a poster to promote your comic book!

Scroll Back

Edit and proofread your legend, paying particular attention to the following:

❏ Have you used hyphens correctly?
❏ Have you appealed to your readers' senses through onomatopoeia or other means?
❏ Have you spelled all words correctly, especially those with a three-consonant pattern?

Unit ③ Biography

What is a biography?

A biography is an account of a person's life written by someone who knew the person or who researched the person's life. Authors of biographies often focus on particular events as a way to reveal the life or personality of the main character. The following incident is taken from *Skywalking: The Life and Films of George Lucas*, a biography of the filmmaker written by Dale Pollock.

It was a June Saturday night in Modesto, California, and the teenagers were cruising McHenry Avenue, leaning out the windows of their souped-up custom cars, yelling to their friends. The traffic was so thick that George and Marcia Lucas had difficulty getting to the Modesto Elks Lodge. Lucas smiled at the familiar scene—he was an original cruiser from 1962. But instead of wearing a white T-shirt and sitting behind the wheel of his Fiat Bianchina, Lucas had on a coat and tie and was driving his $35,000 BMW. You can't stay seventeen forever.

The Lucases were on their way to Thomas Downey High School's twentieth class reunion. George hadn't existed for most of the three hundred attendees when they were in school together—if they remembered him at all, it was as a shy, skinny kid with big ears who got into a terrible car accident just before graduation. But he was the one who had immortalized his classmates in *American Graffiti*. The only other '62 Downey graduate with a claim to fame was Dan Archer, who played a few seasons for the Oakland Raiders. Nobody asked for his autograph.

Know

- the characteristics of a biography
- what phrases are and the function they serve
- some rules for punctuating quotations and dialogue
- common homophones and their meanings

Be Able To

- write a biographical incident
- differentiate some types of phrases
- improve your writing by varying sentence length

Lucas had been looking forward to the reunion, until stories about it began appearing in the newspapers, like the one in the *Los Angeles Times* headlined "Lucas Recalled as a Wimp." Most of the disparaging remarks were made by people who barely knew Lucas, like Dennis Kamstra, a salesman of animal pharmaceuticals—he told a reporter that Lucas was his locker partner, "the kind of wimp you used to slap around with a towel." Lucas was quiet and small, but he insists he was no wimp. "I never got beaten up in school, that's for sure. I had my friends," Lucas says.

The negative comments, whether said in ignorance or envy, should have warned Lucas of what was to come. As soon as he put on the name tag bearing his high school picture, heads turned and voices whispered. Soon George was besieged by autograph-seekers thrusting programs, cocktail napkins, placemats, and business cards at him. Lucas spent much of the evening patiently signing his name for people he didn't even know, the first time so many adults had asked for his autograph. He had naively assumed that the luster of his *Star Wars* fame had worn off.

In a class whose graduates had become teachers and doctors, accountants and pharmacists, real estate and water bed salesmen, George Lucas was a star. "People came up whom I'd gone to school with since I was in kindergarten and said, 'Gee, I don't know whether you'll remember me...' Why wouldn't I remember them? You know somebody for fifteen years, you're not going to forget them," he says.

Checkpoint: Biography

Discuss how these general characteristics of a biography apply to the model. Later, you can use the list to help you revise your own work.

✓ It describes real events.

✓ Although it is based on fact, the author may invent some details.

✓ It is usually chronological.

✓ The events chosen reveal something about the personality or life of the subject.

1. On your own or in pairs, generate a list of at least five people who may be good subjects for a biography. Choose one, and jot down a reason for your choice.

Idea File

Good subjects for a biography might include parents, grandparents, friends, community leaders, or teachers.

2. You may already have a specific incident in mind that you would like to write about. If so, ask your subject to tell you about it. Use the five W's—who, what, where, when, and why—to guide you in asking questions. If you do not know of a particular event to focus on, your interview will have to be more open-ended. Try asking your subject questions about major events in his or her life (births, marriages, travels, schools, deaths) until a particular event emerges that you think would make an interesting topic. Then start asking more specific questions about that event.

3. Arrange the facts in a logical order. Then write a first draft of your biographical incident. Although your work should be solidly based on fact, you can invent dialogue to make your writing more vivid. You can also make up details that you think would be appropriate for the setting, people, and events. Show your draft to your subject and ask him or her to correct any inaccuracies.

4. Revise your work until you are satisfied with its focus, content, and organization.

GRAMMAR

A **phrase** is a group of words that lacks a subject or a verb (or both), but functions as a unit within a sentence.

There are four main types of phrases: noun, verb, adjective, and adverb. Notice how each phrase functions as a single unit in the following sentences.

Subjects are discussed in Unit 5.

noun phrase
Many teenagers were yelling to their friends.

verb phrase
George **hadn't existed** for most of the three hundred attendees.

adjective phrase
Although he was once a **shy and skinny** kid, he grew up to be famous.

adverb phrase
Lucas's biographer **very clearly** believes that his subject is a great filmmaker.

I. Tell whether the italicized word group in each of the following sentences is a phrase. If it is a phrase, tell what kind.

a) *George Lucas almost didn't graduate* from high school.
b) He was in a *very bad* car crash just before graduation.
c) Miraculously, he *did survive* the crash.
d) The incident affected his life *quite profoundly*.
e) *After he recovered,* he took life much more seriously than before.

There are other types of phrases that can act as nouns, adjectives, and adverbs in a sentence.

A **prepositional phrase** begins with a **preposition** and ends with a noun or pronoun.

A preposition is a word that shows the relationship between a noun or pronoun and another word in the same sentence. (For example, the word *with* in *kid with big ears* shows a relationship between *kid* and *big ears*.) Other prepositions include words like *about, across, along, at, before, between, by, from, in, through, of,* and *under.*

A prepositional phrase may act as an adjective or an adverb.

adjective

George was a shy, skinny kid <u>with big ears</u>.

adverb

Lucas smiled <u>at the familiar scene</u>.

2. Find five more prepositional phrases in the model and determine whether they are acting as adjectives or adverbs.

Language Link

MECHANICS

Know

- some rules for punctuating quotations and dialogue

To add interest to a biography, try to include direct quotations from the person you are writing about, or from others who knew him or her. Here are some rules to remember when writing dialogue or quotations.

- Always enclose direct speech in quotation marks.
- Begin quotations with a capital letter.
- Do not use quotation marks with indirect speech.
- Always put commas and periods inside the quotation marks.
- Separate a direct quotation from a speaker's tag *(he said)* by a comma.

1. Working with a partner, make up examples to illustrate these rules.

2. Now look at the following exceptions. In your notebook, complete each exception based on the evidence in the examples.

   a) Dennis Kamstra told a reporter that Lucas was "the kind of wimp you used to slap around with a towel."

      Exception: Do _____ begin a quotation with a _____ _____ if the quoted material is blended into another sentence.

   b) "People," says Lucas, "came up whom I'd gone to school with since I was in kindergarten."

      Exception: If the speaker's tag breaks a sentence in the middle, use a _____ before and after the _____ _____ and do not _____ the first word after the speaker's tag.

40

Techno Tip

When editing on computer, do a global search for an opening quotation mark ("). As each example comes up, check your use of punctuation and capitals against your list of rules.

1. Rewrite the following sentences in your notebook, adding the correct punctuation and capitalization.

   a) Luke, come over to the dark side said Darth Vader
   b) Obi-Wan Kenobi's favourite expression was may the force be with you
   c) Do or do not there is no try says Yoda.

2. Now correct the mistakes in punctuation and capitalization in these sentences, which have been taken from other parts of the George Lucas biography.

   a) You can't have that kind of experience [his near death in a car crash] and not feel that there must be a reason why you're here." Lucas explains. "I realized I should be spending my time trying to figure out what the reason is and trying to fulfill it."
   b) "He only completed the first [Star Wars] trilogy," he says, because "I had a slight compulsion to finish the story."
   c) The newsletter reflected Lucas's whimsical sense of humour (As we stand here in the grease pit of eternity... is how one editorial began).
   d) Lucas told one matronly woman he saw for the first time in twenty years "you told me in my yearbook that I'd be where I am today."

3. Tape record a minute or two of conversation, either real or from television. (You may even want to rent one of the Star Wars movies and use some dialogue from that.) Then write it down, using quotation marks and capital letters where necessary.

4. Try writing your own dialogue. You might want to imagine a conversation between you and one of the Star Wars characters, or between two of the characters in a Star Wars film. Have a classmate proofread your work for correct punctuation. Then, have two volunteers perform the dialogue in front of the class. How realistic does it sound?

Writing

Unit **3** **Biography**

Language Link

USAGE & STYLE

Be Able To

- improve your writing by varying sentence length

Readers can quickly lose interest in passages whose sentences all sound the same. One way to add variety and interest to your writing is to include sentences of different lengths.

1. Working with a partner, read the following passage out loud and discuss how it sounds. Then read the first paragraph of the model out loud. What differences do you notice? Write a short summary of these differences, identifying the effect of varying sentence length.

It was a June Saturday night in Modesto, California. The teenagers were cruising McHenry Avenue. They were leaning out the windows of their souped-up custom cars. They were yelling to their friends. The traffic was thick. George and Marcia Lucas had difficulty getting to the Modesto Elks Lodge. Lucas smiled at the familiar scene. He was an original cruiser from 1962. But he wasn't wearing a white T-shirt. And he wasn't sitting behind the wheel of his Fiat Bianchina. Lucas had on a coat and tie and was driving his $35,000 BMW. You can't stay seventeen forever.

2. Read your biographical incident aloud, checking to see if you have varied the length of your sentences. Ask yourself the following questions.

   a) If my sentences are mostly short ones, where can I join some of them to create a few longer ones?

   b) If my sentences are mostly long ones, where can I break some of them to create a few shorter ones?

SPELLING

Homophones are words that sound alike, but have different meanings and spellings. Most homophones are small, but they are surprisingly troublesome to spell because they are so easily confused.

Words to Watch For

The words below, all taken from the biographical excerpt at the beginning of the unit, may look simple, but watch out—they are all homophones.

night	their	for	one	know
scene	way	been	knew	your

In your notebook, make a list of 8-10 words that are homophones. You can use words from this box, the excerpt, and your personal reading.

1. Write the homophone partner (or partners) for each word in your list. Choose five sets of homophones. For each set, write a sentence that shows the meaning of each homophone (for example, *I was **too** tired **to** read*).

2. The following homophones are frequently misspelled.

   its   it's   to   too   two   there   their

   Practise your skill as a peer editor by looking for the homophones above in a piece of writing by a classmate. (You might work on the draft of his or her biographical incident.) Make sure the homophones are all spelled correctly.

3. There are a number of **mnemonics** (tools that can help your memory) for spelling homophones. For example, *A beach is by the sea, a beech is a kind of tree.* Create a mnemonic that will help you spell homophones. Post your mnemonic with those of your classmates.

Scroll Back

Edit and proofread your biographical incident, paying particular attention to the following checklist:

- ❑ Have you correctly punctuated and capitalized any quotations or dialogue?
- ❑ Have you used sentences of varying length to keep the reader interested?
- ❑ Have you spelled all homophones correctly?

Unit 3 Biography

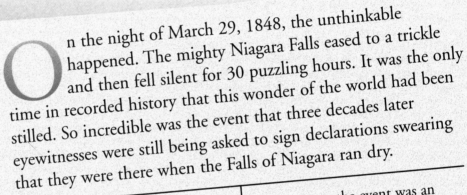

What is a historical narrative?

Historical narratives record information about significant events. Because these events took place in the past, the writer must research them carefully to make sure that he or she records the facts accurately. The following excerpt is from D. W. Phillips' historical narrative entitled *The Day Niagara Falls Ran Dry*.

THE DAY

NIA

On the night of March 29, 1848, the unthinkable happened. The mighty Niagara Falls eased to a trickle and then fell silent for 30 puzzling hours. It was the only time in recorded history that this wonder of the world had been stilled. So incredible was the event that three decades later eyewitnesses were still being asked to sign declarations swearing that they were there when the Falls of Niagara ran dry.

Residents first realized that something was wrong when they were awakened by an overpowering, eerie silence. Inspection of the river by torches revealed only a few puddles of water in the river bed. The next morning, some 5000 sightseers from as far away as Hamilton and Buffalo jammed the roads to Niagara Falls and converged on the riverbank to see the phenomenon. The American Falls had slowed to a dribble, the British Channel was drying fast, and the thundering Canadian Horseshoe Falls were stilled.

For some, the event was an interesting curiosity. Peering down from the bank, they saw long stretches of drying mud, exposed boulders and chains of black puddles. Fish and turtles lay floundering in crevices. While thousands stood in disbelief, a few daredevils explored recesses and cavities at the bottom of the dry river gorge never before visible. They picked up bayonets, muskets, swords, gun barrels, tomahawks, and other relics of the War of 1812. Others took the historic opportunity to cross the river above and below the falls—on foot, on horseback, or by horse and buggy.

At the end of this unit you will

Know
- the features of a historical narrative
- the functions of verbal phrases
- the functions of dashes
- some exceptions to the "**i** before **e** except after **c**" rule

Be Able To
- write your own historical narrative
- differentiate infinitive phrases from prepositional phrases
- use present-tense verbs to create excitement

A FALLS

RAN DRY

For superstitious people, the unusual silence and unexplained phenomenon was a portent of divine wrath or impending doom. As the day wore on, fear and anxiety spread. Thousands attended special church services on both sides of the border. Native people in the area shared in the belief that some disaster was about to happen.

Tension grew until the night of March 31, when a low growl from upstream announced the return of the waters. Suddenly, a wall of water surged down the river bed and over the falls. The deluge quickly covered the massive boulders at the base of the falls and restored the ever-present Niagara spray. Relieved residents relaxed and returned home to sleep again to the rumble and boom of the falls.

The cause of the stoppage, it was discovered later, was an ice jam that had formed on Lake Erie near Buffalo.... The combined force of wind, waves, and lake currents jammed hundreds of thousands of tonnes of ice into a solid dam at the neck of the lake and the river entrance between Fort Erie and Buffalo. Eventually, the ice cut off the water's flow and the basin downstream gradually dried out....

Will Niagara Falls ever run dry again? Probably not, at least not on its own accord. Since 1964, an ice boom has been positioned at the head of the Niagara River every winter to prevent the formation of ice blockages and safeguard hydroelectric installations.

The falls have been turned off, though. For seven months in 1969, the United States Army Corps of Engineers diverted the river to permit repairs to the eroding face of the American Falls. On six other recorded occasions, the American Falls have frozen over completely. February 1947 was especially cold and the channel on the north side of Goat Island, which separates the two falls, became completely blocked with large masses of ice. But not the Canadian Horseshoe Falls. With 10 times the volume of the American Falls, only once has its mighty roar been stilled —on that memorable March night in 1848.

Checkpoint: Historical Narrative

Discuss how these general characteristics of a historical narrative apply to the model. Later, you can use the list to help you revise your own work.

✓ It is usually written in chronological order.

✓ It is based on facts.

✓ The writer knows the outcome, but may hold back information to create interest and suspense.

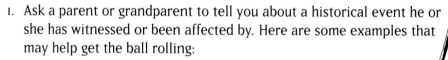

1. Ask a parent or grandparent to tell you about a historical event he or she has witnessed or been affected by. Here are some examples that may help get the ball rolling:

   - world fairs, such as Expo '67 or Expo '86
   - visits by famous persons (Nelson Mandela, the Queen, etc.)
   - World War II (your grandparents might remember it)
   - the first moonwalk
   - a strike or demonstration
   - immigration to Canada from another country

2. Jot down the events that interest you most, and then choose the one you think would make the best historical narrative. Ask your parents or grandparents for their permission to research their participation in this event.

Idea File

As a writer, you have an obligation to respect the wishes of your subject. Do not write someone else's story without his or her permission.

3. On a sheet of paper, make two headings: WHAT I KNOW and WHAT I NEED TO FIND OUT. In the first column, write down all the facts you know about the event. In the second column, list fact-based questions you would like to have answered. Consult reference resources to find the answers to your questions.

4. Arrange an interview with your relative. Before you begin your interview, make a list of questions you have about the event that you think your subject could answer. Concentrate on collecting details that will make your narrative interesting.

5. Write a draft, and ask your subject to read it to check the accuracy of what you have written. Refer back to the Checkpoint, and revise your draft until you are satisfied with its focus, content, and organization.

GRAMMAR

Language Link

Know
- the function of verbal phrases

Be Able To
- differentiate infinitive phrases from prepositional phrases

Subjects are discussed in Unit 5.

A **verbal phrase** is a phrase that contains a verb form that is not the main verb of the sentence.

The verb forms used in verbal phrases usually end in **-ing, -ed, -en,** or **-t.** Verbal phrases usually function as adjectives, but they can also function as nouns within a sentence.

verbal phrase functions as an adjective modifying *they*

Peering down from the bank, they saw long stretches of drying mud, exposed boulders and chains of black puddles.

verbal phrase functions as a noun, the subject of the verb *is*

Leaning over the barrier is a good way to get yourself killed!

Another kind of verbal phrase is the **infinitive phrase**. An *infinitive* is a verb form with the word *to* in front of it, and infinitive phrases can act as nouns, adjectives, or adverbs.

functions as a noun

To cross the Falls on a tightrope is dangerous, but many have tried.

functions as an adjective modifying *boom*

To prevent another ice jam, a boom now sits at the head of the Niagara River.

functions as an adverb modifying *climbed*

People climbed down to recover articles from the War of 1812.

Unit **4** Historical Narrative

For more on prepositional phrases, see Unit 3.

Strategy

Not all phrases that start with *to* are infinitive phrases. Some **prepositional phrases** do as well. You can tell the difference by looking at what kind of word comes directly after the word *to*. If it is a verb form, you are probably dealing with an infinitive phrase.

1. For each of the following sentences, explain whether the phrase in boldface is a prepositional or an infinitive phrase.

    a) **To many people**, the silence was eerie.
    b) They waited anxiously **to hear the familiar roar of the water**.
    c) Those who were brave enough crossed over **to the other side** on foot.

2. Find at least five examples of prepositional or infinitive phrases in the model. For each, explain what kind of phrase it is, and how it functions in the sentence.

MECHANICS

Know

• the functions of dashes

A **dash** (—) is used in a sentence to show an abrupt change. It emphasizes the importance of the information that follows it.

Here are two versions of the same sentence: one with and one without the dash.

> Others took the historic opportunity to cross the river above and below the Falls—on foot, on horseback, or by horse and buggy.

> Others took the historic opportunity to cross the river above and below the Falls on foot, on horseback, or by horse and buggy.

1. With a partner, discuss the difference in emphasis between the two sentences. What effect does the dash have?

Sometimes writers use a *pair* of dashes to separate material from the rest of the sentence.

Erosion has slowly pushed Niagara Falls upstream—the Canadian Falls recedes about 1.5 metres every year and the American Falls recedes about 15 centimetres—and this has formed the Niagara Gorge.

2. Below are two pairs of sentences. Rewrite each pair as a single sentence, using a pair of dashes to include information from the second sentence in the first.

   a) The Niagara's large volume of flow and its steep drop make it an important source of hydroelectric power. Approximately 5520 cubic metres of water flow over the Falls every second.

   b) Millions of people come each year to see the Falls, and a popular site for many of them is the Cave of the Winds near the base of the American Falls. Visitors come from all over the world.

3. Write three more sentences using a pair of dashes. Read the sentences out loud to your partner, or rewrite them on a piece of paper without the dashes, and have a partner figure out where the dashes should go.

Techno Tip

Instead of using two hyphens (--) to create a dash, most word-processing programs allow you to print a single, long dash (—) known as an em-dash. Look in your manual to find out how to create an em-dash in your program.

USAGE & STYLE

Language Link

Be Able To
- use present-tense verbs to create excitement

Writers often use the present tense to generate excitement and tension because it makes readers feel they are there watching the event happen. Note the effect of each of these sentences.

Past: Suddenly, a wall of water surged down the river bed and over the falls.

Present: Suddenly, a wall of water surges down the river bed and over the falls.

Unit 4 Historical Narrative

Idea File

Although some writers intentionally mix both past and present verb tenses to create a particular effect, it is important not to mix tenses unnecessarily or by mistake.

1. Rewrite the following passage, correcting any inappropriate shifts in tense.

Hurricane Hazel hit Toronto on the evening of October 15, 1954. Since hurricanes rarely if ever reach this far north, nobody was prepared for its arrival. The result was a disaster for many residents of Toronto.

On that fateful evening, the hurricane winds are blowing at 120 km an hour. A cold front is moving in the opposite direction, and when it met the warm tropical air from the west it produced torrential rains. Low-lying areas like Holland Marsh were completely flooded, and some streets near the banks of the Humber River are submerged in a matter of minutes: some residents die and many others are left homeless as houses slip off of foundations and were carried away, with their occupants clinging desperately to the roofs.

SPELLING

Know

- some exceptions to the "**i** before **e** except after **c**" rule

You've heard the rule "**i** before **e** except after **c**." It's a helpful rule—you've probably used it many times as you wrote words that contain **ie**. There are times, however, when this rule can't help you. What about words like *weigh* or *science*? In this mini-lesson, you will learn about some exceptions to the "**i** before **e**" rule.

Words to Watch For

All of these words contain **ei** or **ie** combinations. Some have been taken from the historical narrative at the beginning of the unit.

eerie	anxiety	scientific	brief	conscience
disbelief	relieved	yield	perceive	vein

In your notebook, make a list of 8-10 words that contain **ie** or **ei** combinations, focusing on words that are tricky to spell because they don't follow the usual pattern. You can use words from this box, the narrative, and your own reading.

1. Write the words in your list that contain each of the patterns below. If you have no lesson words that match, work with a partner to find an example. Include the word(s) from each pattern in a sentence. Be creative! Write each sentence as if it were part of an exciting historical narrative—but one that comes from your own imagination. (For example, *The people of Palookaville stared in disbelief as the Mounties raced madly towards the frontier.*)

   a) When **i** and **e** combine to form the **long e** sound, **i** comes before **e** (for example, *believe*).

   b) When **i** and **e** combine to form the **long a** sound, **e** comes before **i** (for example, *weigh*).

   c) When **i** and **e** combine to make a **long** or **short i** sound, **e** comes before **i** *(height, foreign).*

Strategy

Some words do not follow rules or patterns. Keep a list of words like these in your Personal Dictionary. Highlight the letters that make each word difficult to spell.

2. There are exceptions to every rule. Find an exception to the patterns listed above.

3. Words that contain **ient** or **ience** patterns do not fit any of these rules. This is because the two vowels do not combine to make one sound (for example, *science*). Include one of these words in a sentence from an (imaginary) historical narrative.

4. Working in groups, choose one of the patterns in question 1. List as many words as you can that follow the pattern. As a class, create a chart that shows the rules related to **i** and **e**. Include the words that cause the most spelling difficulties, drawing from the examples listed by each group.

Scroll Back

Edit and proofread your historical narrative, paying particular attention to the following checklist:

❏ Have you used dashes appropriately?
❏ Have you used verb tenses consistently, switching only when necessary to achieve a certain effect?
❏ Are all words spelled correctly? Pay special attention to words that contain **i** and **e** combinations.

Unit 4 **Historical Narrative**

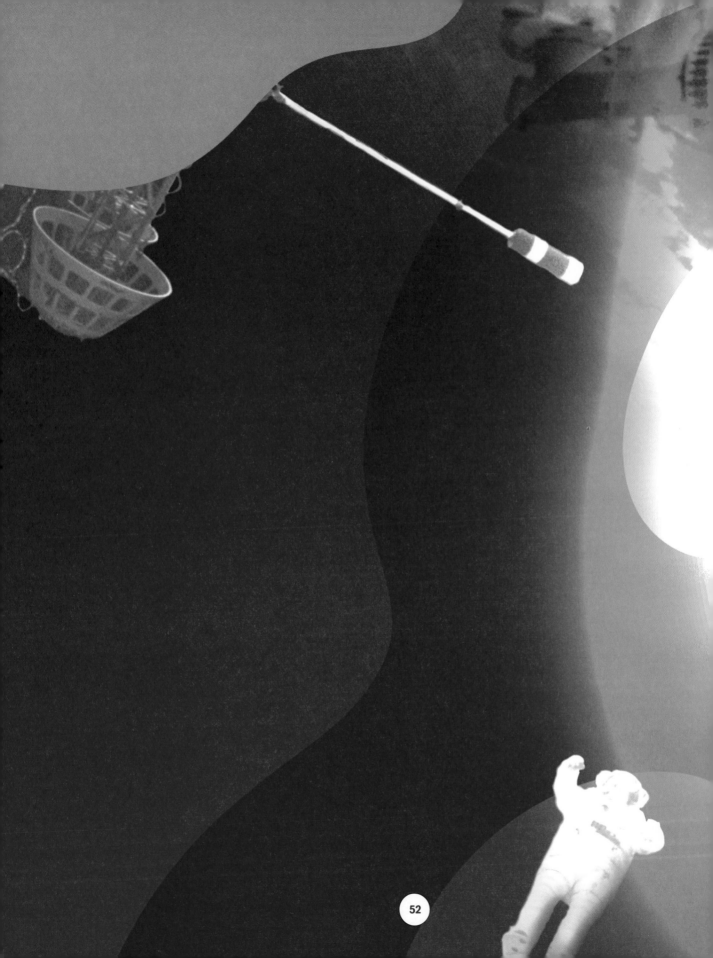

Description

"It looked like ...."

"It sounded like ...."

Whether the subject is a person, place, object, or even an idea, description involves choosing details that convey a specific impression. For example, while you're likely to describe your favourite music video using words that convey a particular image, your parents or grandparents might choose words that convey quite a different image.

This section contains four forms of descriptive writing: travelogue, lyric poetry, character sketch, and place description. Through careful selection and presentation of details, each piece paints a vivid impression of its subject, helping us to experience places, people, even feelings, through someone else's eyes.

Features of Description

- Descriptions focus on creating a dominant impression of a person, place, feeling, or idea.

- Descriptive writers choose words, images, and details that appeal to more than one sense, and that reinforce the dominant impression they want to give their readers.

- Descriptive writing often uses figurative language techniques such as simile and metaphor.

- Descriptions may be organized in various ways; for example, spatially, in time sequence, or by comparison.

Unit ⑤ Travelogue

What is a travelogue?

A travelogue is a description of a journey or trip. The purpose may be to convince readers to take the trip themselves or simply to describe what the writer experienced while travelling. The following "Canadian Rockies Sampler," an ad that has been downloaded from the Internet, takes the form of a travelogue.

Forward   Reload   Home   Search   Guide

Location: **http://www.roadslesstraveled.com/**

Merging the peace of alpine hiking, the western flair of horseback riding, and the thrill of backwoods biking and white-water rafting, Roads Less Traveled has created an exciting combo-adventure that features the best of Canada's mountain parks: Banff, Jasper, Yoho, and Kananaskis. Keeping in mind a range of abilities, we've put together a week of active days and luxurious nights sure to satisfy your appetite for adventure and relaxation.

Our travels begin in Kananaskis Country, a dazzling region south of Banff that many consider to be one of Canada's finest secrets. Rolling out the mountain bikes, we glide carefree and alone past shimmering peaks mirrored in emerald lakes.

That evening, we loosen up our legs in the outdoor hot tub at the Mt. Engadine Lodge, a European-style retreat secluded in a lush valley rimmed by rugged snow-shrouded pinnacles.

Heading to Lake Louise, we don a knapsack, lace up the hiking boots, and get ready for two days of footloose fun in the Plain of Six Glaciers and the remarkable Iceline Trail. Located in lightly-traveled Yoho National Park, the Iceline is a classic route that contours the edge of Emerald Glacier, offering unique close-up views of a glacial environment. Our inspiring days are complemented with nights of heavenly comfort at the

At the end of this unit you will

Know
- the characteristics of a travelogue
- when to use italics, underlining, or quotation marks in titles
- how words are affected by the addition of suffixes

Be Able To
- write a travelogue
- recognize the simple and complete subject and the simple and complete predicate
- use alliteration to create a mood or to appeal to the reader's senses

n Lake Louise and the Canadian Rocky Mountain

 Print   **Security**   **Stop**

historic Deer Lodge, featuring gourmet dining and an idyllic setting.

We then swing into the saddle for a morning horseback ride to Bow Falls. That afternoon, we are accompanied for a hike in Jasper by Ben Gadd, author of *Handbook of the Canadian Rockies* and an acknowledged authority on the region. Our destination is Wilcox Pass, noted for its panoramic vista of the Columbia Icefield. Mountain heather and delicate alpine tundra carpet our footpath as we keep a sharp lookout for bighorn sheep and other wildlife. More incredible glacier views greet us from our rooms that evening at the Icefield Chalets, spectacularly set at the toe of the Athabasca Glacier.

For the finale of our Rocky Mountain extravaganza, we return to our bikes for a day of scenic cycling on the renowned Icefields Parkway and then board rafts for a white-water thriller on the mighty Kicking Horse River.

Techno Tip

Advertisers on the World Wide Web need to create excitement for their products through words. Web advertisers know that many people will not wait for a gorgeous graphic or photograph to download; they want information right away, so words have to do the job.

WRITER'S WORKSHOP

Checkpoint: Travelogue

Discuss how these general characteristics of a travelogue apply to the model. Later, you can use the list to help you revise your own work.

✓ It describes a place that the author has visited personally, and may include pictures.

✓ Its purpose may be to convince readers to visit the place described.

✓ It normally describes events in the order in which they happened.

✓ It focuses on aspects of the trip or location that will be of particular interest to readers.

✓ It often uses techniques such as onomatopoeia and alliteration to convey strong sense impressions.

1. Make a list of places you have been that you know or remember well. Suitable subjects for a travelogue might be an interesting neighbourhood in your hometown, or a place you visited on holiday recently. From your list, choose a place that you think your peers might find interesting to read about.

2. Write a sentence in which you identify your topic, your purpose for writing, and your audience.

3. Make a chart like the one below, and fill it with as many details as you can remember about your trip. (Not all the categories may be appropriate to your subject.)

Sights	Sounds	Smells	Sensations	Tastes

4. Write a first draft of your travelogue. Remember to emphasize details that will interest your particular readers.

5. Revise your writing until you are satisfied with its focus, content, and organization.

GRAMMAR

At the heart of every sentence is a noun or pronoun (the **simple subject**) and a verb (the **simple predicate**).

simple subject   simple predicate
Rolling out the mountain bikes, <u>we</u> <u>glide</u> carefree and alone.

simple subject   simple predicate
<u>Roads Less Traveled</u> <u>has created</u> an exciting combo-adventure.

simple subject   simple predicate
Our <u>travels</u>   <u>begin</u> in Kananaskis Country.

The **complete subject** includes the simple subject and all the words that modify it. The **complete predicate** includes the simple predicate and all the words that modify it.

complete subject   complete predicate
<u>Our destination</u>   <u>is Wilcox Pass.</u>

complete subject   complete predicate
<u>We</u>   <u>swing into the saddle for a morning horseback ride.</u>

complete subject   complete predicate
<u>More incredible glacier views</u>   <u>greet us from our rooms.</u>

Strategy

To find the subject, ask who or what the sentence is *about*. To find the predicate, ask yourself what the subject is *doing* or what the sentence is *telling* us about the subject.

1. In your notebook, write the main noun and the main verb in each of the sample sentences above.

Unit **5** Travelogue

2. Copy the following sentences, labelling the simple subject (SS) and simple predicate (SP), and underlining the complete predicate.

   a) We return to our bikes for a day of scenic cycling.
   b) Heading to Lake Louise, we don a knapsack.
   c) Located in Yoho National Park, the Iceline is a classic route that contours the edge of Emerald Glacier.
   d) Mountain heather carpets our footpath.

3. Try drawing the following sentences in the form of a web. Draw a circle for the main noun and another for the main verb. Then cluster the other words in the sentence around whichever word they seem to modify, or explain. For example:

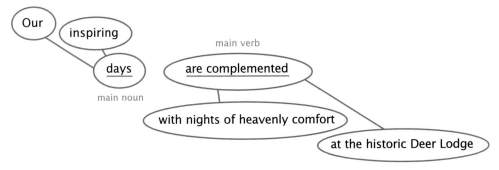

   a) Keeping in mind a range of abilities, we have put together a week of active days and luxurious nights.
   b) That afternoon, we are accompanied for a hike in Jasper by Ben Gadd, author of *Handbook of the Canadian Rockies* and an acknowledged authority on the region.
   (Hint: The subject isn't always found at the beginning of the sentence.)

4. In your notebook, add words to the following noun/verb pairs to create original sentences. Identify which words belong to the subject, and which to the predicate. Working in groups of three or four, see who can come up with the longest subject or predicate, or who can create the funniest sentence.

   a) mountains   soar   b) rattlesnakes   hiss   c) feet   ache

5. A sentence that is missing either a simple subject or a simple predicate is called a **sentence fragment**. In your notebook, correct the following sentence fragments by adding either a subject or a predicate or both. Add proper punctuation.

For more information on sentence fragments, see Unit 10.

a) Tourists, dropping garbage as they went.
b) The great brown bear hidden in the cave.
c) Without looking fell head first into the hot tub.
d) Skillfully avoided plunging over the cliff.
e) Lacing my boots and buttoning my jacket carefully.

MECHANICS

Italics and quotation marks (" ") are used to set off titles. Underlining is used in place of italics in handwritten work.

Know
· when to use italics, underlining, or quotation marks in titles

That afternoon, we are accompanied for a hike in Jasper by Ben Gadd, author of *Handbook of the Canadian Rockies* and an acknowledged authority on the region.

Use italics (underlining) for …	Use quotation marks for …
books	chapters
plays	short stories
magazines and newspapers	articles in magazines or
long poems	newspapers
musical compositions (operas,	short poems in a collection
symphonies, etc.)	songs
films	TV episodes

I. Find three *real* examples of each of the kinds of titles listed on the chart. (You may want to visit the library for this activity.)

A Challenge
Can you think of a general rule of thumb that explains most of the differences between titles that are italicized and those that are put in quotation marks? Try to express the difference in one sentence, then create a sign or slogan to remind the class of the rule.

USAGE & STYLE

Be Able To

- use alliteration to create a mood or to appeal to the reader's senses

To catch their readers' interest, travel writers often use techniques such as onomatopoeia (see Unit 2) or alliteration. Alliteration means using words that begin with similar sounds. Repeating soft sounds like **m** or **v** can create a feeling of peace and tranquillity (for example, *misty mountains, velvety valleys*). Hard sounds like **b** or **t** emphasize action and excitement (for example, *backwoods biking, tiger tracking*).

1. With a partner, take turns reading the "Canadian Rockies Sampler" out loud, paying attention to the author's use of alliteration. What effect does the author seem to want to create with his or her use of alliteration?

2. Check through your travelogue, and look for places where you might use alliteration or onomatopoeic words to create a mood or emphasize a strong sense impression.

3. Choose one of the following products and write two advertising slogans to describe it. Use hard alliteration in one slogan and soft alliteration in the other.

toothbrush	wristwatch	telephone
stereo	running shoes	in-line skates

Which slogan do you prefer? Why?

SPELLING

Know

- how words are affected by the addition of suffixes

A suffix is a word part that is added to the end of a word. The function of a word is partly determined by the suffix that is attached:

- a noun can become a verb   *softness*   *soften*
- a verb can change its tense   *soften*   *softened*
- a verb can become an adjective   *soften*   *soft*
- an adjective can become comparative   *soft*   *softer, softest*
- an adjective can become an adverb   *soft*   *softly*

Suffixes like **-s, -ed,** and **-ing** can change the tense of a verb, while **-er** and **-est** can be added to adjectives or adverbs in order to make comparisons.

Words to Watch For

Each of these words has a suffix and has been taken from the travelogue at the beginning of the unit.

merging	relaxation	mirrored	offering	acknowledged
luxurious	loosen	secluded	accompanied	inspiring

In your notebook, list 8-10 words that have a suffix and that can be difficult to spell. You can use words from this box, the travelogue, and your personal reading. To help you learn the words, underline their suffixes.

1. Underline the root of each word in your list. Group your words according to whether the word stayed intact or lost a letter when the suffix was added. What generalization can you make about words that lose a letter when a suffix is added?

2. In your notebook, write the **Words to Watch For** that match these definitions.
   a) a verb that can be an antonym for *fasten*
   b) an adjective that can be a synonym for *isolated*
   c) a past-tense verb that can be a synonym for *went with*
   d) an adjective that can be a synonym for *uplifting*

3. Develop a class list of words that end in a suffix. List the words under these headings: NOUNS, VERBS, ADJECTIVES, and ADVERBS. Underline the root in one colour and the suffix in another.

4. From the travelogue at the beginning of the unit, choose six words that you find unfamiliar or interesting. The words should be nouns, verbs, adjectives, or adverbs. Give your list to a partner, challenging him or her to change the part of speech of each word by either adding or deleting a suffix. Your partner should use each new word in a sentence. Complete the same task with your partner's words.

Scroll Back

Edit and proofread your travelogue, paying particular attention to the following:

❏ Have you used italics and quotation marks correctly in titles?
❏ Have you used alliteration or onomatopoeia to create a mood or emphasize a sense impression?
❏ Are all words spelled correctly, especially those containing suffixes?

Unit **5** **Travelogue**

Unit 6 — Lyric Poetry

What is lyric poetry?

Just as there are different kinds of prose, there are different kinds of
poetry. Narrative poetry, for example, tells a story, while lyric poetry
emphasizes feelings.

ALONE

The feeling of being left out—
Not liked by anyone
Where your throat is dry
And your lips feel like the rough bark
  of the tree,
Your rough lips stick together
And won't open,
Just like an old door stuck
In the doorway.
Where your eyes, like the walls of a weir
Won't open because
If they do
The walls will burst
And the water will rush out.

— Sue Kitchin

Know

- the characteristics of a lyric poem
- the difference between simile and metaphor
- some digraphs and the sounds they make

Be Able To

- write your own lyric poem
- distinguish between linking and action verbs
- choose the correct modifier for a linking or action verb
- use contractions correctly

WRITER'S WORKSHOP

Checkpoint: Lyric Poetry

Discuss how these general characteristics of lyric poetry apply to the model. Later, you can use the list to help you revise your own work.

✓ The story is secondary to the feelings the poet wants to convey about the subject.

✓ The poet uses line breaks and punctuation as well as words to convey meaning.

✓ A lyric poem usually includes similes, metaphors, alliteration, and onomatopoeia in order to create strong sensory impressions.

✓ It may be written in rhyme or free verse, which tries to capture the flow of natural speech and does not rhyme.

1. Below are a few writing prompts. In your notebook, respond to each of them using as few words as possible. **Do not name the thing you are writing about**—just describe each experience as clearly as you can in a few words or a phrase.

    · the sound of footsteps walking behind you in a dark street
    · the feeling of an icy breeze sweeping across the back of your neck
    · the sound of a door with rusty hinges opening slowly
    · the taste of medicine you dislike
    · the sound of fingernails clawing a blackboard
    · the feeling of getting popcorn stuck in your throat and not being able to breathe

2. In activity 1 above, you created several images that might convey to a reader what fear is like. Put a check mark beside the ones you feel do the best job of showing what it is like to feel afraid.

3. Think of these images as lines of a poem called "Fear." Read the images you checked one more time and, on another sheet of paper, arrange them in an order that pleases you. Refer back to the Checkpoint to guide you as you arrange your words.

4. Read your poem aloud twice. Add words or phrases you think are needed to connect ideas or to make your poem easier to read. Delete words or phrases you think are not needed. Add a final line if you think your poem needs one.

5. Read your poem one more time, paying close attention to its appearance on the page. Decide whether you want to combine lines or break them in different ways. Poetry does not have to follow the same rules that other forms of writing follow, so feel free to capitalize and punctuate your poem in your own way. Just remember that the *way* you present your poem should help readers see your subject the same way you do.

GRAMMAR

Be Able To
- distinguish between linking and action verbs
- choose the correct modifier for a linking or action verb

A **linking verb** links a subject with an adjective that describes the subject.

	action verb	adverb
She	spoke	dryly.

	linking verb	adjective
Your throat	is	dry.

Most verbs are *action* words, and writers use *adverbs* to modify them. However, *linking verbs* do not show action, and are used only to link adjectives to the nouns they modify.

Verbs like *appear, seem, grow,* and *become,* and verbs associated with the senses *(look, sound, smell, feel,* and *taste),* are often used as linking verbs, so they should be followed by adjectives. However, they can also be used as action verbs, so writers need to be careful what modifiers they use after them.

1. Choose the correct modifier in each of the following sentences. Explain your choices.

   a) A stranger appeared *(quiet, quietly)* from nowhere.
   b) The boy appeared *(quiet, quietly)* after the frightening ordeal.
   c) I felt *(nervous, nervously)* about entering the dark, deserted house.
   d) I felt *(nervous, nervously)* around in the dark for a light switch.

Strategy
If you have difficulty deciding which type of modifer to use, try replacing the verb with a form of the verb *be.* If the meaning of the sentence stays the same, the verb is a linking verb, so use an adjective after the verb.

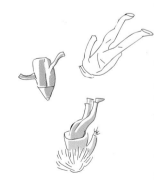

2. Copy the following sentences in your notebook, correcting any mistakes in the use of modifiers.

Chilly fingers feel icily along my neck. Must be the wind. I feel badly that I didn't bring a scarf. Suddenly, the fingers seem differently: more like human fingers. I scream loud and run quick for the shelter of my house. In the street, a shadow appears briefly and then is gone.

3. Choose three linking verbs. Write two sentences for each verb: one sentence that uses it as a linking verb (followed by an adjective), and one sentence that uses it as an action verb (followed by an adverb).

Idea File

Linking verbs are often very useful. However, writers usually prefer to use action verbs in order to make their writing more forceful.

4. Look through the draft of your poem, as well as two or three journal entries or other pieces of writing you have completed recently. Correct any mistakes in the use of linking verbs and modifiers, and decide whether any of the linking verbs could and should be replaced with an action verb.

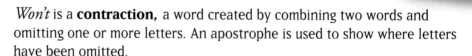

MECHANICS

Be Able To
- use contractions correctly

Where your eyes, like the walls of a weir
Won't open

Won't is a **contraction,** a word created by combining two words and omitting one or more letters. An apostrophe is used to show where letters have been omitted.

1. What two words have been combined to form *won't?*

2. Why do you suppose the author used this contraction instead of the two separate words?

Formal and informal language are discussed in Unit 14.

3. Contractions are more acceptable in informal writing than in formal writing. Look through your writing portfolio and find one piece of writing that is less formal and one that is more formal. Have you used contractions correctly and appropriately in both?

USAGE & STYLE

One way to describe something clearly is to compare it to something that has similar characteristics. Because lyric poems deal with feelings and emotions, which are sometimes hard to describe, they usually make use of various **figurative language** techniques to create the right mood. **Simile** and **metaphor** are comparisons between things that are unlike in nature.

A **simile** is a *direct* comparison using *like* or *as.*

Sue Kitchin uses several similes in her poem, and one of them appears in the following line:

> And your lips feel like the rough bark of the tree

This simile could also have been written using *as* to make the same comparison (*And your lips feel as rough as the bark of the tree*).

1. Identify the other two similes in Sue Kitchin's poem. Which do you think is the best comparison? Why?

Strategy

When similes get overused, they no longer have much impact. They become clichéd. (For example, *as fit as a fiddle, as right as rain, bright as a new penny, as hard as nails.*) Avoid clichés like the plague. (Oops!) Try to think of fresh images that will get your audience's attention.

2. Write sentences that contain similes describing each of the following scenarios. Remember to avoid clichés, and to create similes that will show readers exactly how you see and feel about these experiences.

a) a crowded bus
b) the minute before an exam starts
c) a traffic jam
d) the first morning of summer vacation
e) a starless night
f) a field covered with fresh snow

A **metaphor** is an *implied* comparison.

Writers create metaphors in a number of ways. One way is to state that one thing or experience is the same as another. For example,

> The sun was a yellow ball on the horizon.

Writers can also imply comparisons by choosing modifiers and verbs that suggest qualities related to other things. Note the metaphors that appear in the following sentences:

The deer paused beside the emerald lake.

Emerald compares the colour of the lake to the green gem.

When Lina saw the note from her teacher, her good mood evaporated.

Evaporated compares Lina's mood to a liquid that vanishes quickly.

3. Explain the metaphor in each of the following sentences by identifying what the writer is comparing.

   a) The narrow road snaked through the mountain pass.
   b) A spidery network of wires stretched from one tower to the next.
   c) The schooner plowed through the frothy waves.

4. Look back at your poem on fear. Have you used fresh, accurate similes and/or metaphors to create comparisons? If not, do you want to include any to illustrate your experience?

Writing

SPELLING

Know

• some digraphs and the sounds they make

Digraphs are two letters that combine to make a new sound. They differ from blends, where the sounds of both letters can be heard.

Words to Watch For

Some of these words include roots from the lyric poem at the beginning of the unit. The others are words you might use in your poetry. All of the words contain digraphs.

roughly	rushes	anguish	mischievous	sympathy
wherever	authentic	enthusiasm	astonishment	physical

In your notebook, make a list of 8-10 words that have a digraph and that can be difficult to spell. You can use words from this box, the lyric poem, and your personal reading. To help you learn the words, underline the digraph in each word.

1. Which digraphs does your word list contain? Create a chart with these digraphs across the top. Under each digraph, list four words that contain the digraph. Try to choose examples that show each digraph in a different position (at the beginning, in the middle, and at the end of a word).

2. The word *mischievous* is often misspelled. Think of a way you can help others spell the word. Write your tip on a piece of paper that your teacher can display with other tips written by your classmates.

Strategy

To learn difficult words try visualizing them. Write the word, look at the letters that make it up, then cover the word. Picture the word in your mind and write what you see. Then uncover the word and compare the two. Did visualizing help you spell the word? If not, try the strategy again. If yes, try the strategy using another word.

3. Use each of these word pairs in a sentence.

   a) roughly   wherever
   b) astonishment   mischievous
   c) rushes   sympathy

4. Compound words are two words that have been combined to make a new word. The meaning of the new word is drawn from the two words that make it up. One of the **Words to Watch For** is a compound word. Work with a partner to list ten other compound words that contain a digraph. Use these words to create a crossword puzzle for your classmates.

Scroll Back

Edit and proofread your poem, paying particular attention to the following:

❏ Have you used the correct modifier with any linking verbs?
❏ Have you used action verbs whenever possible?
❏ Have you used contractions correctly and appropriately?
❏ Have you used fresh, accurate similes and metaphors to make your images more compelling?
❏ Are all words spelled correctly? Pay special attention to words that contain digraphs.

Unit **6** Lyric Poetry

Unit (7) Character Sketch

What is a character sketch?

A character sketch paints a portrait of a real person or a fictional character, using words that convey a clear impression of physical appearance and personality. The following character sketch is taken from the novel *Obasan* by Joy Kogawa.

Obasan

She is an old woman. Every homemade piece of furniture, each pot holder and child's paper doily, is a link in her lifeline. She has preserved in shelves and in cupboards, under layers of clothing in closets—a daughter's rubber ball, colouring books, old hats, children's dresses. The items are endless. Every short stub pencil, every cornflake box stuffed with paper bags and old letters is of her ordering. They rest in the corners of the house like parts of her body, hair cells, skin tissue, food particles, tiny specks of memory. This house is now her blood and bones.

She is all old women in every hamlet of the world. You see her on a street corner in a village in southern France, in her black dress and her black stockings. She is squatting on stone steps in a Mexican mountain village. Everywhere she stands as the true and rightful owner of the earth, the bearer of love's keys to unknown doorways, to a network of astonishing tunnels, the possessor of life's infinite personal details.

"I am old," she says.

These are the words my grandmother spoke that last night in the house in Victoria. Grandmother was too old then to understand political expediency, race riots, the yellow peril. I was too young.

Know

- the characteristics of a
  character sketch
- what an antecedent is
- what pronoun to use with
  indefinite antecedents such as
  anybody or *someone*
- how to use parallel structures
  for items in a series and within
  a sentence to emphasize ideas

Be Able To

- write a character sketch
- make pronouns agree with
  their antecedents
- use capital letters
  appropriately
- form possessives for singular
  and plural nouns

Joy Kogawa

She stands up slowly. "Something in the attic for you," she says.

We climb the narrow stairs one step at a time carrying a flashlight with us. Its dull beam reveals mounds of cardboard boxes, newspapers, magazines, a trunk. A dead sparrow lies in the nearest corner by the eaves.

She attempts to lift the lid of the trunk. Black fly corpses fall to the floor. Between the wooden planks, more flies fill the cracks. Old spider webs hang like blood clots, thick and black from the rough angled ceiling....

I use the flashlight to break off a web and lift the lid of the trunk. A strong whiff of mothballs assaults us. The odour of preservation. Inside, there are bits of lace and fur, a 1920s nightgown, a shoe box, red and white striped socks. She sifts through the contents, one by one.

"That's strange," she says several times.

"What are you looking for?" I ask.

"Not here. It isn't here."

She turns to face me in the darkness. "That's strange," she says and leaves her questions enclosed in silence.

WRITER'S WORKSHOP

Checkpoint: Character Sketch

Discuss how the characteristics of a character sketch apply to the model. Later, you can use the list to help you revise your own work.

✓ Aspects of personality may be revealed through physical detail, setting, objects, action, dialogue, or observers.

✓ The sketch may begin with a single overall impression of the character, then provide details to support this impression.

✓ The sketch may also be written as a narrative, or story, in time sequence.

1. Choose a subject for a character sketch. Your character can be real or fictional. For example, you might consider writing about one of the following:

   - a superhero
   - a character from your favourite TV show
   - a character you make up
   - a member of your family or community
   - a friend

2. Write your subject's name at the top of a blank page. Below it, write the following headings, and fill in details that might help to reveal your character's personality.

Physical Detail	A scar or a missing tooth or soft, pale hands can create an immediate impression.
Setting	Placing a person in the boardroom of a major corporation or in a shelter for the homeless immediately shapes the reader's perception of the person.
Objects	Giving the character an object like an expensive watch or a ridiculous handbag will help generate an image of that person. It is not only the item itself but also what the person does with it that helps show what he or she is like.
Action	A character's actions (for example, kicking a dog or helping an old man cross a street) reveal something about his or her personality.
Dialogue	The type of language the person uses and the things he or she says reveal a lot about the person.
Observers	In real life, as in literature, we learn much about people from what others say about them.

3. Using the details you listed above as a guide, decide on a scene or incident that will serve as the basis for your character sketch. Arrange your details in a logical order, and write a first draft of your sketch.

4. Give your draft to a friend to comment on. Refer back to the Checkpoint, and revise your piece until you are satisfied with its focus, content, and organization. Have you managed to paint an accurate picture of your subject?

GRAMMAR

Pronouns must agree with their **antecedents**.

The antecedent is the noun the pronoun refers to.

plural antecedent → plural pronoun

The <u>items</u> are endless.... <u>They</u> rest in the corners of the house like parts of her body.

1. Under the heading PRONOUNS, list all the personal pronouns in the excerpt from Joy Kogawa's *Obasan*. Under the heading ANTECEDENTS, list the antecedent of each pronoun.

Use a **singular pronoun** to refer to the antecedents *each, every, neither,* or *either,* or a word ending in *-body* or *-one* (for example, *somebody, no one*).

2. Read the following sentences, and in your notebook write the correct pronoun for each antecedent. In each case, explain why you chose that particular pronoun.

a) During the Second World War, anybody in Canada who was of Japanese ancestry lost *(his or her; their)* right to freedom.

Know

- what an antecedent is
- what pronoun to use with indefinite antecedents such as *anybody* or *someone*

Be Able To

- make pronouns agree with their antecedents

73

Unit 7 Character Sketch

b) Many Japanese Canadians in B.C. were held in detention camps against *(his* or *her; their)* will.

c) Joy Kogawa and her family were among the many who lost *(his* or *her; their)* property.

d) Each of the characters in Kogawa's book, *Obasan*, suffers greatly from *(his* or *her; their)* internment.

e) No one can read the book without increasing *(his* or *her; their)* understanding of this important episode in Canadian history.

> Using the male pronouns *he, him,* or *his* to refer to an antecedent that could be either male or female is considered **gender bias** by many people, and should be avoided.

3. Find three ways to rewrite the following sentence to avoid gender bias.

   Each student will receive his report card on the last day of school.

4. Evaluate your use of pronouns in your character sketch. Are there any mistakes in pronoun-antecedent agreement? Have you avoided gender bias wherever possible?

5. Look through some other pieces of writing you have recently completed and take note of any errors you tend to make with pronouns. Then design a reminder page in your notebook to help you avoid making similar mistakes in the future.

Language Link

MECHANICS

Be Able To
- use capital letters appropriately

1. Copy the following sentence from the excerpt and circle the words that are capitalized. Then explain why each is capitalized. (Can you explain why the word *grandmother* is *not* capitalized here?)

   "I am old," she says. These are the words my grandmother spoke that last night in the house in Victoria.

2. Working with a partner, write at least three other rules that explain when you should use capital letters.

3. Look through your character sketch and make any changes to capitalization you think are necessary. If you found errors, think of a rule that can help you to avoid making the error again.

USAGE & STYLE

Items in a list or series must be **parallel** in structure.

When items in a list or series are parallel, they are balanced. Each item may be a word, a phrase, or a clause. The more closely they resemble each other, the more balanced the sentence will be.

Parallel: Grandmother was too old then to understand
<u>political expediency</u>, <u>race riots</u>, <u>the yellow peril</u>.
     noun phrase   noun phrase   noun phrase

Not Parallel: Grandmother was too old then to understand <u>what was politically expedient</u>, <u>race riots</u>, <u>the yellow peril</u>.
     clause   noun phrase   noun phrase

Know
- how to use parallel structures for items in a series and within a sentence to emphasize ideas

Phrases are discussed in Unit 3, and clauses are discussed in Unit 9.

Idea File
Repeating a structure in a passage makes it stand out, so parallelism adds emphasis to an idea.

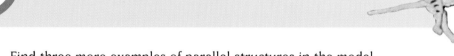

1. Find three more examples of parallel structures in the model.

2. Writers use parallelism to create a particular effect in a passage. What effect do you suppose Joy Kogawa hoped to create in the second paragraph of the excerpt? Explain why you think this.

3. Correct the following sentences by making elements within them parallel.

    a)   His nose was red, his eyes were blue, and he had a full head of white hair.

    b)   Nadia slammed the door, threw her schoolbag in the general direction of the cupboard, and her body slumped down on the couch.

    c)   The dog went everywhere with her: to market, to the hairdresser, even when she went visiting, much to her friends' dismay.

    d)   The house, like its inhabitant, was big, old, and rambled on.

Language Link

SPELLING

Be Able To

- form possessives for singular and plural nouns

Making a noun possessive usually involves adding **'s**. You can find two examples in the excerpt from *Obasan:*

Singular Noun	child	daughter
Possessive Form	child's paper doily	daughter's rubber ball

To make a plural noun possessive, usually you only have to add an apostrophe (') , since the word already ends in **s.** When a noun is an irregular plural, however, this rule does not apply. You can see the difference in the following two examples.

	regular plural	irregular plural
Plural Noun	boxes	children
Possessive Form	boxes' contents	children's dresses

 Words to Watch For

Some of the words listed below have been taken from the *Obasan* excerpt; others have been added to provide more examples of possessive forms.

child's	children's	people's	tenants'	profession's
daughter's	astronaut's	women's	architects'	prisoners'

In your notebook, make a list of 8-10 possessive nouns that can be difficult to spell. Use words from this box, the character sketch, and your personal reading.

1. Review your word list. Circle words that are plural possessives and underline irregular plural possessives. How many of your words are singular possessives?

Strategy

Print each **Word to Watch For** on a strip of paper. Fold the paper like an accordion so that each fold contains one syllable. Spell the word aloud as you unfold each syllable.

2. Rewrite each phrase in your notebook, using the correct possessive form. (For example, *the attic of the woman* → *the woman's attic.*)

   a) the corners of the house
   b) the contents of the trunk
   c) the dull beam of a flashlight
   d) every hamlet of the world
   e) the steps of the stairs
   f) the smell of mothballs

3. Choose three **Words to Watch For** and include each in a different sentence.

4. Write two sentences, each containing a possessive. In one sentence the possessive should be singular, and in the other it should be plural. Cut your sentences so that each word is on a separate piece of paper. Mix all the pieces and give them to a partner to reconstruct.

Scroll Back

Edit and proofread your character sketch. As you edit, pay particular attention to the following checklist:

❏ Do your pronouns agree with their antecedents?
❏ Have you avoided gender bias in your use of pronouns?
❏ Are all items in a list or series written with similar grammatical elements?
❏ Have you used parallelism to emphasize ideas where appropriate?
❏ Do all possessives have the proper form?
❏ Are all words spelled correctly, including possessives?

Present It!

Draw a picture or include a photograph of your subject to accompany your character sketch.

Unit 7 Character Sketch

Unit 8 Place Description

What is a place description?

While descriptions of locations are often written as part of a longer work, many can also stand on their own. When describing a place, writers carefully select details that convey a *dominant impression*, such as the elegance of a mansion, the loneliness of a deserted farmhouse, or the eeriness of a graveyard at night. The following description is taken from W. O. Mitchell's novel *Who Has Seen the Wind?*

WHO HAS SEEN THE WIND?

Here was the least common denominator of nature, the skeleton requirements simply, of land and sky—Saskatchewan prairie. It lay around the town, stretching tan to the fat line of the sky, shimmering under the June sun and waiting for the unfailing visitation of wind, gentle at first, barely stroking the long grasses and giving them life; later, a long hot gusting that would lift the black topsoil and pile it in barrow pits along the roads, or in deep banks against the fences.

Over the prairie, cattle stood listless beside the dried-up slough beds which held no water for them. Where the snow-white of alkali edged the course of the river, a thin trickle of water made its way toward the town low upon the horizon. Silver willow, heavy with dust, grew along the riverbanks, perfuming the air with its honey smell.

Know

- the characteristics of a place description
- how compound words are written
- the meaning of the term **schwa vowel** and the sound these vowels make in words

Be Able To

- describe a place you know
- use *who* and *whom* correctly in a sentence
- use personification to enhance your writing style

W.O. MITCHELL

Just before the town the river took a wide loop and entered at the eastern edge. Inhabited now by some eighteen hundred souls, it had grown up on either side of the river from the seed of one homesteader's sod hut built in the spring of eighteen seventy-five. It was made up largely of frame buildings with high, peaked roofs, each with an expanse of lawn in front and a garden in the back; they lined avenues with prairie names: Bison, Riel, Qu'Appelle, Blackfoot, Fort. Cement sidewalks extended from First Street to Sixth Street at MacTaggart's Corner; from that point to the prairie a boardwalk ran.

Lawn sprinklers sparkled in the sun; Russian poplars stood along either side of Sixth Street. Five houses up from MacTaggart's Corner stood the O'Connal home, a three-storied house lifting high above the white cottage to the left of it. Virginia creepers had almost smothered the veranda; honeysuckle and spirea grew on either side of the steps. A tricycle with its front wheel sharply turned stood in the middle of the walk.

WRITER'S WORKSHOP

Checkpoint: Place Description

Discuss how these characteristics of a place description apply to the model. Later, you can use the list to help you revise your own work.

✓ Details are chosen to support an overall, dominant impression.

✓ It usually follows a consistent visual pattern (for example, the place is described from left to right, outside to inside, or top to bottom).

✓ Impressions are often described using figurative language techniques, such as simile, metaphor, onomatopoeia, alliteration, or personification.

✓ The description usually contains details that appeal to the different senses.

✓ It is usually written from the narrator's point of view.

1. Think of places you could describe clearly and list them in your notebook. Although W. O. Mitchell describes a whole community, begin by identifying single locations—your backyard, even your room—that you know well.

2. Look at the places you have listed and put a check mark beside those you know best. Then, beside each one, try to identify the *dominant impression* you have of that place. If you cannot associate a dominant impression with a particular place, cross it off your list. From those remaining, choose one you would like to describe.

3. Write the following headings in your notebook: SIGHT, HEARING, SMELL, TASTE, and TOUCH. List as many details under each heading as you can. Then cross off those that do not help to convey the dominant impression you are aiming for. (For example, one student identified the beach as a peaceful place to be, so she decided not to include details about screeching sea gulls and barking dogs.)

Idea File

If possible, visit the place you are going to be describing. Bring a notebook or tape recorder and write down or record your impressions while you are there.

4. Imagine you are a cinematographer shooting background footage for a movie. Choose one of the following ways of shooting your footage, and write a draft of your description following that order.

   - You could pan across the place from left to right, or from right to left, or from top to bottom, or from bottom to top.
   - You could begin by filming the whole place in a wide-angle shot and then move in to focus on a particular thing. (This is what W. O. Mitchell does in his description.)
   - You could focus on one thing and then pull back to reveal the whole place in a wide-angle shot.

5. Refer back to the Checkpoint, and revise your draft until you are satisfied with its focus, content, and organization.

GRAMMAR

Be Able To
- use *who* and *whom* correctly in a sentence

Use **who** as a subject; use **whom** as an object.

Many students have difficulty knowing when to use the pronouns *who* and *whom.* Do you know which form of the pronoun to use in the following sentences?

(Who, Whom) brought Maria to the Prairies?

She brought Maria, so use *who.*

(Who, Whom) did you visit in Saskatchewan?

We visited *him* there, so use *whom.*

Strategy

When *who* or *whom* appears at the beginning of a question, answer the question in a sentence using *he/she* or *him/her.* If you use the subject pronoun *he/she* in your answer, choose the subject pronoun *who.* If you use the object pronoun *him/her* in your answer, choose the object pronoun *whom.*

Unit **8** Describing a Place

1. Write the correct pronoun in each sentence below.

   a) *(Who, Whom)* drove across the Prairies last summer?
   b) *(Who, Whom)* were you planning on visiting?
   c) *(Who, Whom)* gave you W. O. Mitchell's novel to read on the trip?
   d) *(Who, Whom)* did you leave the book with when you finished it?

When *who* and *whom* are used in the middle of a sentence, look at the verb following the pronoun to determine if you require a subject pronoun *(who)* or object pronoun *(whom)*.

> My grandmother, **who died last year,** lived in this house for 89 years.

In the part of the sentence following the pronoun, the verb *died* has no subject, so use the subject pronoun *who.*

> My grandfather, **whom** *I apparently resemble,* built this house himself.

In the part of the sentence following the pronoun, the verb *resemble* already has a subject *(I),* so use the object pronoun *whom.*

2. Write the correct form of each pronoun in your notebook. Give a reason for your choice.

   a) W. O. Mitchell is an author *(who, whom)* many people associate with the Prairies.
   b) The main character is a young boy living on the Prairies, *(who, whom)* we watch growing up.
   c) Was it Pierre Berton *(who, whom)* once called W. O. Mitchell "an original"?

3. Go back through your writing and evaluate your use of *who* and *whom*. Analyze the kinds of mistakes you find, and think of a way to avoid making the same mistakes in the future.

Language Link

MECHANICS

Know
- how compound words are written

Words become part of our language in many ways. One way is through **compounding,** in which two existing words are put together to form a new word.

> Silver willow, heavy with dust, grew along the **riverbanks,** perfuming the air with its honey smell.

Compound nouns are sometimes written as one word, sometimes written as two, and sometimes hyphenated. If you are unsure how to write a particular compound word, check its spelling in a dictionary.

There is no simple rule for writing compound nouns, since the same word may undergo many changes. For example, you might see any of the following words in contemporary writing: *prize fighter, prize-fighter,* and *prizefighter.* Generally speaking, the longer a compound noun is in use, the more likely it will be written as one word. When choosing a particular form of a word, be sure to be consistent within a piece of writing.

A compound adjective that appears before the noun it modifies is usually hyphenated.

1. Rewrite each of the following in your notebook using a compound adjective. (For example, *a hat with a wide brim* would become *a wide-brimmed hat.*)

   a) a boy who is four years old
   b) a relationship between a father and a son
   c) a job that can be done by one person
   d) a telephone call that is made over a long distance
   e) a story that has been written well

2. Find four more examples of compound words in the passage from *Who Has Seen the Wind?*

USAGE & STYLE

Be Able To
- use personification to enhance your writing style

> Later, a long hot gusting ... would lift the black topsoil and pile it in barrow pits along the roads.

In this sentence, Mitchell creates the impression that the wind is almost human. This is **personification**, a special comparison in which a writer gives human qualities to something that is not human. Just like simile and metaphor, personification can help emphasize specific details and, therefore, make a passage more interesting for a reader.

1. Find at least two other examples of personification in the excerpt. Explain the comparison in the examples you have found.

Unit 8 Describing a Place

Writers create personification by choosing modifiers, verbs, and even nouns that suggest qualities related to human beings.

The sailor cast a worried glance at the angry sea.

The adjective *angry* refers to a human emotion.

A breeze whispered through the trees.

The verb *whispered* is an action that people perform.

The first snow of the year left its signature at the edge of the field.

The noun *signature* refers to something that people create.

2. Write five sentences that each use personification to create a vivid image of a particular place. Try to vary the mood of your sentences; for example, they can be funny, or dramatic, or haunting.

3. Advertisers often use personification to emphasize a particular quality of a product. Look through magazines and newspapers and find several examples of personification. Clip or photocopy the ads, mount them neatly on unlined paper, and place in a duotang. Below each ad, explain the personification the advertiser has used.

4. Look back at your place description and see if you can increase its effectiveness by using personification. Rewrite a portion of the piece using this type of comparison.

SPELLING

Know
- the meaning of the term **schwa vowel** and the sound these vowels make in words

A **schwa vowel** is a vowel sound that occurs in an unstressed syllable. For example, say the word *description* (dĭ skrĭp′shən). As you can see from the pronunciation in brackets, the middle syllable is stressed, while the first and last syllables are not. The final unstressed syllable is pronounced with a neutral "uh" vowel sound, known as a schwa (ə). Words that contain the schwa vowel sound can be difficult to spell because the sound doesn't belong to a particular spelling pattern.

Words to Watch For

These words, taken from the description at the beginning of the unit, are pronounced with the schwa vowel sound.

denominator	alkali	visitation	horizon	homesteader
requirements	trickle	inhabited	sparkled	middle

In your notebook, make a list of 8-10 words that you think have at least one schwa vowel sound and that can be difficult to spell. You can use words from this box, the description, and your personal reading.

1. Write five of your words in your notebook. Say each word aloud, then write the syllables you hear. Mark the stressed syllable using the stress mark ('), and represent the schwa vowel using this symbol (ə). When you have finished, check your work in a dictionary, making corrections where necessary.

 Strategy

Link patterns in words you are learning to spell to patterns in words you know how to spell. For example, knowing how to spell *tickle* can help you spell *trickle* or *tackle*. Linking patterns can help you spell words that are difficult to sound out.

2. Work with a partner. Trade the corrected word lists you completed in question 1 above. On separate, small pieces of paper write the syllables of the words, one syllable per piece. Jumble the papers and give them to your partner. Can she or he put the pieces together to make the original words?

Scroll Back

Look back through your description of a place. Edit and proofread it, paying particular attention to the following points:

❑ Have you used *who* and *whom* correctly?
❑ Have you looked up any compound nouns in the dictionary to check how they are spelled? Have you spelled them consistently throughout the piece?
❑ Have you used figurative language, including personification, to create vivid images?
❑ Are all words, especially those containing schwa vowels, spelled correctly?

Unit 8 **Describing a Place**

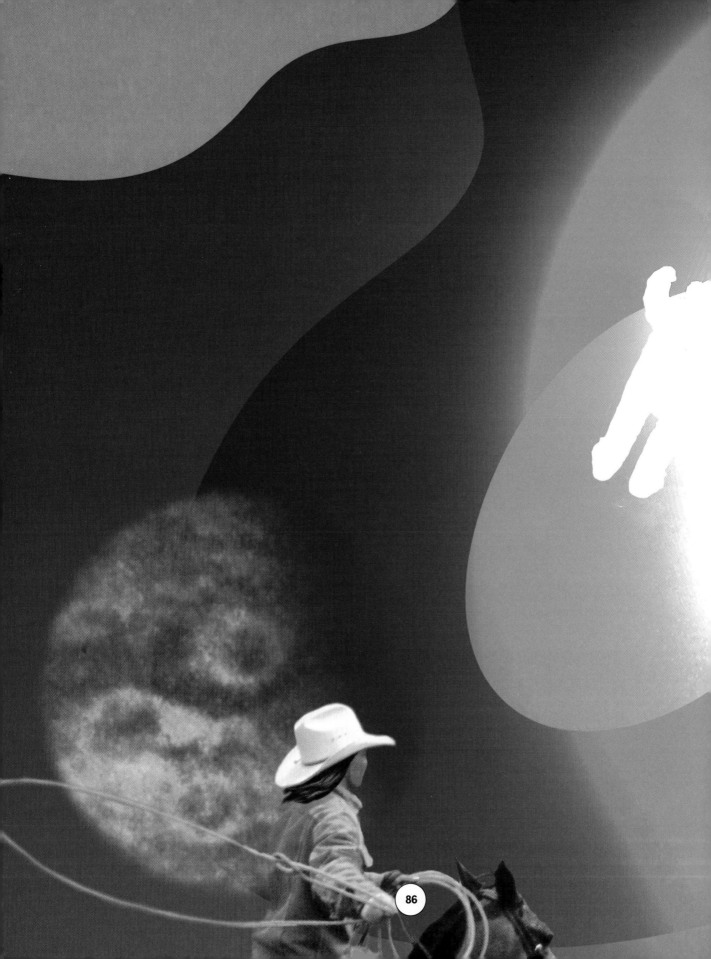

Exposition

Expository writing surrounds us. Car repair manuals, self-help books, basketball rule guides, recipes—any writing that communicates facts is exposition. It's writing that tells who, what, when, where, why, and how. But if you've ever been frustrated by badly written instructions, you'll know that good expository writing involves more than simply presenting facts. It's crucial that these facts be organized in order to meet the needs of the reader.

This section contains four forms of expository writing: instruction, comparison, definition, and hard news story. Although these forms are very different from one another, each presents factual information about a process, idea, or event in a format that's useful and understandable to the reader.

Features of Exposition

- Exposition involves presenting facts to a specific audience.

- Expository writing is arranged in whatever way is most useful to the reader.

- Expository writers often draw comparisons with something more familiar as a way of making new information understandable to their audience.

- The writer's personal opinions and value judgments aren't usually part of expository writing.

Unit 9 Instructions

What are instructions?

One of the most common forms of exposition is writing that presents instructions for how to do something. Whether they involve tying shoelaces or building a nuclear reactor, instructions need to be stated clearly and arranged in an order that is easy for a reader to follow. The following set of instructions is entitled "Measure Yourself."

Sometimes, your natural shape and abilities aren't what a certain sport was designed for; other times, it's as though the sport were sewn just to fit you. In between, there are all sorts of clothes—er, sports—that may not be an exact fit, but that look pretty good with a little altering or a few accessories.

So how do you know if a sport fits you? You could try it on—work at it for a while, see if you're good at it. Or you could, in a way, hold it up to yourself and see—roughly—if it matches your natural shape and abilities. How can you "hold it up to yourself"? With a bit of measuring!

Try Your Lungs on for Size

You'll need the following:
a big plastic bag (such as a kitchen garbage bag)
a marker that will write on the bag
a funnel
a container (such as a pitcher) marked off in litres (or quarts)

1. Bunch together the opening of the bag to make a mouthpiece, the way you would with a paper bag you were planning to blow up and burst. Make the mouth opening wide so you can breathe into the bag with your mouth open.
2. Squeeze the bag to let the air out.
3. Hold the bag away from your mouth and take two normal slow breaths.
4. On the next breath, breathe in as much air as you can; then bring the plastic bag to your mouth.

Know

- the characteristics of instructions
- the difference between independent and subordinate clauses
- when to use a semicolon
- what a diphthong is
- some of the patterns that make the **oi** and **ou** sounds

Be Able To

- write your own set of instructions
- identify transitional expressions that indicate a time sequence, a contrast, or a spatial relationship

5. Pinch your nose and breathe out hard in one breath into the bag. Keep your mouth open—don't purse your lips as though you were blowing. Continue pushing the air out until you feel as though every last drop of air is squeezed from your lungs. (Hint: It helps to bend forward as you breathe out.)

6. Close the bag tightly and hold it while you take it away from your mouth.

7. Slide your hand down the neck of the bag until the bag is completely expanded. Mark the bag at the point where you're holding it in case your grip slips.

8. Push the neck of the funnel into the mouth of the bag, still keeping a firm hold on the bag so it doesn't move. Don't worry about the air escaping—you don't need it.

9. Using the marked container, carefully pour water into the bag until it's as fully expanded with water as it was with air. The bag will get quite heavy, so you may want to rest it on something as you fill it.

This will give you an approximate idea of your lung capacity. The average 137 cm (4 foot 6 inch) tall boy has a lung capacity of approximately 2 L (2 quarts). The average 152 cm (5 foot) tall girl has a lung capacity of about 2.7 L (3 quarts).

Compare your lung capacity to that of friends who are the same sex and height as you are. If you have a greater than average lung capacity, you have an advantage in endurance sports, like cross-country skiing, or long-distance running or swimming. For short, intense bursts of energy, like sprinting, large lung capacity probably isn't as important—many sprinters hardly breathe at all during the few seconds they're racing.

Checkpoint: Instructions

Discuss how these characteristics of instructions apply to the model. Later, you can use the list to help you revise your own work.

- ✓ Their purpose is to show the reader how to perform a set of actions.
- ✓ They usually begin with a brief introduction, along with a list of tools or ingredients needed to perform the task.
- ✓ Steps in the process are often numbered.
- ✓ They are arranged in the same order in which the actions are performed.
- ✓ They may be accompanied by graphics.

1. Make a list of things you know how to do. Circle the things that would be useful to learn for a reader who is five years younger than you, and choose one that you feel would be interesting to explain.

2. If possible, perform the activity yourself, and jot down information you will include in your instructions as you go. (For complex parts, consider supplementing your words with a graphic.) Also prepare a list of materials needed to perform the task. Then write a first draft.

3. Refer back to the Checkpoint as you revise. If possible, get someone from your target audience to try following your instructions. Keep revising your set of instructions until you are satisfied with its focus, content, and organization.

Know
- the difference between independent and subordinate clauses

> **Clauses** are groups of words that contain a subject and a predicate.

Clauses and phrases are both groups of words that function as units within a sentence; however, phrases do not contain both a subject *and* a verb, while clauses do.

1. In your notebook, indicate which of these are clauses and which are phrases.

   For more on phrases, see Units 3 and 4.

   a) so how do you know
   b) if a sport fits you
   c) to let the air out
   d) using the marked container

subordinate clause   independent clause

If you have a greater than average lung capacity, you have an advantage in endurance sports.

> An **independent clause** makes a complete thought and can stand alone as a sentence. A **subordinate clause** cannot stand alone as a sentence.

Subordinate clauses begin with **subordinating conjunctions,** such as *although, because, before, since, unless, until, while, when, as, if, as if, who, which, that, after,* and *though.*

And, or, nor, for, but, so, and *yet* are **coordinating conjunctions.** They are used to join two independent clauses together.

2. In your notebook, indicate whether the clauses you found in question 1 are independent or subordinate. Find three more of each type of clause in the model.

Strategy

When writing instructions, keep the main action you want performed in an independent clause. Put qualifying information in a subordinate clause following the main clause.

subordinate clause   *no action* in main clause

Weak: As you continue pushing air out, you will *feel* as though every last drop of air is squeezed from your lungs.

main clause with *main action*   subordinate clause

Better: *Continue* pushing the air out until you feel as though every last drop of air is squeezed from your lungs.

3. Read through your instructions and underline the subordinate clauses. Evaluate their use and placement. Can you change any sentences to make the important actions stand out more?

Unit **9**   **Instructions**

MECHANICS

Know

- when to use a semicolon

A **semicolon (;)** is used between two independent clauses to show that they are closely related.

Sometimes, your natural shape and abilities aren't what a certain sport was designed for; other times, it's as though the sport were sewn just to fit you.

1. Explain why you think the writer of this sentence used a semicolon instead of a period or a comma. Then write two more sentences that use semicolons for the same reason.

A semicolon is often used before adverbs like *however, nevertheless, on the other hand, conversely,* and *therefore.*

However, **do not** use a semicolon between independent clauses that are joined by *and, or, nor, for, but, so,* or *yet.* These coordinating conjunctions already show that the sentences are related.

Keep a firm hold on the bag, but don't worry about letting air escape.

Don't worry about letting air escape; however, keep a firm hold on the bag.

2. Consider the two sentences above. What difference do you notice in emphasis? Which do you think would work better in writing instructions? Read through your draft, and revise any similar sentence structures.

3. Join each of the following pairs of sentences in your notebook, using either a comma or a semicolon. Explain the reasons for your choices.

   a) A hammer is fairly useful. But not when it makes violent contact with your thumb.
   b) She told me to blow up the paper bag until it exploded in my face. I asked myself why I should follow that instruction.
   c) I did want to complete the experiment. Nevertheless, I valued my right arm.

Use semicolons to separate items in a series when a comma has already been used.

I have sisters living in Medicine Hat, Alberta; Moose Jaw, Saskatchewan; and Winnipeg, Manitoba.

4. In your notebook, punctuate the following sentence using commas and semicolons.

Slowly she got out the coffee beans filter and pot the butter jam and bread and the jellybeans marshmallows and gumballs.

5. Write a sentence using some or all of the following words. Punctuate your sentence using both commas and semicolons. (Use your imagination! Write a correct sentence that's as long, interesting, weird, or funny as possible.)

Sundre   Alberta   fell off   St. John's   Newfoundland   taxi
Toronto   Ontario   midnight   diner

USAGE & STYLE

Be Able To

- identify transitional expressions that indicate a time sequence, a contrast, or a spatial relationship

One way to help your readers follow the sequence of your instructions is to number them. Another method is to use **transitional expressions,** words or phrases that signal the connection between sentences.

1. Read the following passage and identify as many transitional expressions that indicate a sequence as you can.

My father is the world's worst fisherman—it even says so on the hat we bought him last Father's Day. However, last summer he discovered a sure-fire way of catching fish. You, too, can bring home the big ones if you follow these simple instructions. First, check to see if your equipment is working properly. After all, you don't want to hook a prize fish only to watch your rod and reel disintegrate in your hands. Also, be sure to find a large bucket to hold your monster catch. Next, you need the correct bait. Forget about worms, fancy flies, and lures that cost more than a Rolex—instead, go to your cupboard and take out a small can of corn. (Those of you who don't keep corn on hand will have to make a quick trip to the corner store.) Then, open the yellow pages of your telephone directory, turn to the "U" section, and search for the number of the nearest "U-Fish" location. Once you've found it, dial the number and, when someone answers, check to see if they're open. If they are, ask for directions to their location. The only thing between you and your trophy trout now is a car ride. And don't forget the bucket.

Unit **9** **Instructions**

2. Suggest other transitional expressions that could be used

   a) to arrange details in time sequence (for example, *then*)
   b) to introduce a contrasting point (for example, *however*)
   c) to indicate spatial relationships (for example, *on the left*)

3. Look back at a recent piece of your own writing and see if there are places where you could have used some of the transitional expressions you have worked with here.

SPELLING

Know

- what a diphthong is
- some of the patterns that make the **oi** and **ou** sounds

In some words, such as *boil* and *about*, two vowel sounds combine to make a new sound. The sound that **oi** makes in *boil* and the sound that **ou** makes in *about* are known as **diphthongs.** You can see from the chart below that different patterns make the **oi** and **ou** diphthongs.

oi	ou	oy	ow
oil	sound	joy	cow
voice	out	annoy	frown

Notice that the **oi** and **ou** patterns are usually found in the middle of words, while the **oy** and **ow** patterns can be found in the middle or at the end of words.

Words to Watch For

Some of these words are based on roots used in the instructions at the beginning of the unit. All contain the **oi** or **ou** diphthongs listed above.

mouthpiece	pointless	uncoiled	loyalty	poised
however	outermost	whereabouts	employable	accounted

In your notebook, make a list of 8-10 words that contain a diphthong and that can be difficult to spell. You can use words from this box, the instructions, and your personal reading. To help you learn the words, underline each diphthong.

Strategy

One way to remember a word's spelling is to find a word within the word. For example, if you have trouble spelling the word *poised*, it might help to remember that *poised* contains the word *is*. Make up a simple sentence containing both words (for example, *She is poised*).

1. Look over your word list. If possible, find a smaller word in each of the words. Make up simple sentences that each contain the longer and shorter word. Use these sentences as a reminder when you have to spell the words.

2. Trade word lists with a partner. Write each other's lesson words, leaving blanks for the vowels that make the diphthong. Trade lists again and fill in the blanks in your own list.

3. Read the instructions at the beginning of the unit again, looking for words that contain the diphthongs **oi** and **ou.** In your notebook, write the words. Organize them according to their sounds, and then add three more words to each group. Compare your findings with those of a partner.

4. In your notebook, write the **Words to Watch For** that correspond to the following:
   a) a synonym for *at the edge*
   b) a synonym for *faithfulness*
   c) an antonym for *awkward*
   d) an antonym for *purposeful*

Scroll Back

Edit and proofread your instructions, paying particular attention to the following checklist:

❏ Have you put the main actions to be performed in independent clauses?
❏ Have you used semicolons correctly?
❏ Have you used appropriate transition words (or numbering) to make the sequence of your instructions clear?
❏ Are all words spelled correctly, especially those that contain the diphthongs covered in this unit?

Techno Tip

You may want to use a computer graphics program to make diagrams to accompany your instructions.

Unit **9**   Instructions

Unit ⑩ Comparison

What is a comparison?

When writers compare two people or things or events, they identify what is similar and what is different about them. Comparing something unfamiliar with something more familiar is a good way to help your audience understand something new. The following comparison, by Vicki McKay, is entitled "The Earthride."

It took thousands of years

for people to understand the relationship between the sun and the earth, and to figure out what makes day and night, seasons and climates. Now that we understand it, we can see examples and models of the earth/sun relationship in everyday life. You can find a ride at most amusement parks, for instance, that's called something like "the Octopus." If you can picture our planet circling the sun as if it were on the end of an invisible arm, then this kind of ride is a good model of the relationship between the earth and its sun. Our planet spins like a top at the same time that it circles around the sun at the center of its orbit.

If you've ever been on the Octopus, you know that part of the fun is the fact that your body is going through two different motions at the same time: the seat you're sitting in is spinning around a pole that attaches it to the arm, and then the arm is circling around the center. Let's call Earth's trip through space "the Earthride," and we'll take it a few steps further.

At the end of this unit you will

Know

- the characteristics of a comparison
- when sentence fragments are acceptable
- several uses for apostrophes
- the correct spelling of words containing **r**-controlled vowels

Be Able To

- write a comparison
- avoid using sentence fragments unintentionally
- avoid using apostrophes where only a plural is needed
- differentiate *your/you're; whose/who's; its/it's*

Most octopus rides dip up and down as they circle around the center, but the Earthride stays level the whole way around. Most of them have many arms, all the same distance from the center and all moving together. But the eight other arms on the machinery of the Earthride (each one represents one of the other planets in our solar system) all move separately and at different distances from the center. Right now we are concerned with only one of the arms, and that, of course, is the one we're on.

The spinning seats on other octopus rides usually stay level with the arm and dip and climb with the ride. But our planet is attached to the Earthride at a slant, and while the arm stays level all the way around, the planet on the end is always tilted in the same direction. If you understand the tilt of our planet on the Earthride, then you have the key to understanding its seasons.

Not only is the pole that our planet spins around (called the *axis*) attached to the arm at a slant, but no matter where the planet is on its journey around the center of the ride, the axis remains tilted in the same direction.... Sometimes the bottom part of the planet is tilting toward the center, and at other times the top part is tilting in.

In the real Earthride, one year is the period of time it takes for the earth to make one complete trip all the way around its sun. When the bottom part of the planet, or the South Pole, is tilted toward the sun, then that part gets more heat and light and is experiencing what we call summer. At the same time that the South Pole is tilted toward the sun, the North Pole is tilted away from it; it is in shadow and is experiencing winter.

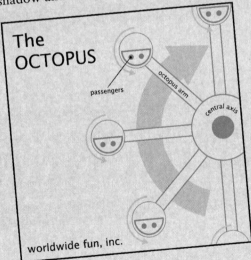

The OCTOPUS

passengers

octopus arm

central axis

worldwide fun, inc.

Checkpoint: Comparison

Discuss how these characteristics of a comparison apply to the model. Later, you can use the list to help you revise your own work.

✓ It is based on direct observation, analysis, or research.

✓ The purpose of a comparison may be to point out the similarities and differences between two objects or ideas, or simply to make something new more understandable by comparing it with something familiar.

✓ The objects or ideas being compared must have some features in common, as well as some differences.

✓ Comparisons are usually organized according to the block method or the point-by-point method (see below).

1. Make a chart like the one below, and fill it in with possible subjects for a comparison (some are already included, to get you started). List as many pairs as you can. When you have finished, choose one pair that you know the most about.

People	Places	Actions	Things
Michael Jordan /Wayne Gretzky	my old house/ my new house	rollerblading/ skateboarding	sneakers/sandals

2. In your notebook, write the ways your subjects are similar. Then note how they are different. Include as many details as you can in both lists.

3. Put a check mark beside at least three similarities and differences you think would help your imagined audience to understand the new subject better. (If you have fewer than three similarities or differences, you need either to brainstorm others or to choose a new subject.)

4. Decide whether you will use the block method or the point-by-point method to organize your comparison.

   • In the **block method,** one item is discussed completely before discussion moves on to the other item (for example, one paragraph

on the popularity, safety, and cost of snowboarding, and then another on the popularity, safety, and cost of skiing).

- In the **point-by-point method,** you might have one paragraph on the popularity of both snowboarding and skiing, another on the safety of both sports, and so on.

Arrange the details, and write a draft.

5. Refer back to the Checkpoint, and revise and edit your comparison until you are satisfied with its focus, content, and organization.

GRAMMAR

A **sentence fragment** is a group of words that is punctuated as a sentence, but that is not a complete thought.

Usually a sentence fragment lacks either a subject or a predicate, or both.

lacks both subject and predicate

The earth spins round the sun. <u>Just like a carnival ride.</u>

lacks subject

It just keeps spinning and spinning. <u>Never slows, never stops.</u>

lacks predicate

Who wants to ride on the Octopus? <u>John.</u>

However, sometimes fragments can have both a subject and a predicate, and still be incomplete:

The spinning seats on other octopus rides usually stay level with the arm and dip and climb with the ride. **But our planet is attached to the Earthride at a slant, and while the arm stays level all the way around, the planet on the end is always tilted in the same direction.**

The sentence in boldface is a fragment because it begins with a coordinating conjunction *(but)* that does not join what follows it *(our planet is attached to the Earthride at a slant)* with anything else in the sentence.

Know
- when sentence fragments are acceptable

Be Able To
- avoid using sentence fragments unintentionally

Subordinating conjunctions are discussed in Unit 9.

Although sentence fragments are grammatically incorrect, writers often use sentence fragments on purpose to create a particular effect. Compare the two examples below. Which passage is more effective in creating drama and tension? Why?

Ben Connors had never been afraid to stay alone until now.

Ben Connors had never been afraid to stay alone. Until now.

1. There is one more sentence fragment in "The Earthride." Can you find it? Why do you suppose the author used a sentence fragment instead of writing the passage another way?

2. Rewrite each of the following fragments as complete sentences. Working with a partner, describe the sorts of changes you had to make to create complete sentences.

   a) The television blaring in the background.
   b) Leaping from rock to rock in the swollen river.
   c) Because I felt terrible.
   d) Under the left cushion of the blue sofa.
   e) Before the dance ended and the music stopped.

3. Choose a piece that you have written recently and read it to find any *unintentional* sentence fragments. Copy any you find in your notebook and then rewrite each fragment as a complete sentence.

4. Tape-record a conversation. Transcribe the tape and analyze the dialogue, looking for sentence fragments. What do you notice about how we use sentence fragments in oral language? Use this information to help you the next time you want to write realistic dialogue.

MECHANICS

Know
- several uses for apostrophes

Be Able To
- avoid using apostrophes where only a plural is needed

Let's call **Earth's** trip through space "the Earthride," and **we'll** take it a few steps further.

Use **apostrophes** to form contractions and possessives. **Do not** use apostrophes to form plurals—except for numbers written as numerals and in cases when omitting the apostrophe may cause confusion.

BOUND

The **skater's** blades made figure **8's** in the ice.

In her handwriting, **e's** and **i's** often look the same.

1. Is the apostrophe used to form a contraction or a possessive in each of the following sentences? Write the answers in your notebook.

For more on contractions, see Unit 6.

   a) The amusement park's attendance increased this year.
   b) All three amusement parks' attendance increased this year.
   c) The amusement park's closing down in the fall.

Strategy

Often the main difficulty students have with apostrophes is knowing when *not* to use them. Always ask yourself if an apostrophe is necessary before using one.

2. Rewrite these sentences in your notebook, correcting any errors in the use of apostrophes.

   a) Hes the only one whose been buying ticket's for the rides'.
   b) Its best not to eat any hotdog's before getting on the Octopus ride.
   c) The earths on a tilt? Well, that explain's the kind of day Iv'e had.
   d) What a trip this years' been! But were all back whe're we started.

USAGE & STYLE

Language Link

Some of the most common word usage problems occur with **homophones** that contain apostrophes. (Homophones are words that sound the same, but are spelled differently.)

> Part of the fun is the fact that **your** body is going through two different motions at the same time: the seat **you're** sitting in is spinning around a pole.

1. Working with a partner, explain the difference between *your* and *you're* in the above passage. Then write a sentence of your own, using each of them correctly.

2. Two other pairs of homophones that create similar problems are *its/it's* and *whose/who's*. Write two sentences, each containing the correct use of one of these pairs.

Be Able To
- differentiate *your/you're, whose/who's, its/it's*

Unit **10** Comparison

Language Link

SPELLING

Know

- the correct spelling of words containing **r**-controlled vowels

Words that contain **r**-controlled vowels can be difficult to spell because the patterns can make a similar sound. Say the following words aloud, listening for the sound made by the **r**-controlled vowels.

coll**ar**   rath**er**   f**ir**   pall**or**   b**ur**dened

 Words to Watch For

Some of these words have been taken from the comparison at the beginning of the unit, while the others are based on roots used in the comparison. All the words contain at least one **r**-controlled vowel.

circling	concerned	experiencing	solar	picturing
orbit	similar	machinery	understanding	earthy

In your notebook, make a list of 8-10 words that contain at least one **r**-controlled vowel and that can be difficult to spell. You can use words from this box, the comparison, and your personal reading. To help you learn the words, underline letters that make the **r**-controlled vowel sound in each word.

Strategy

Since you cannot rely on sound cues to spell words that contain **r**-controlled vowels, you need to learn them in other ways.
1. Practise writing a word by hand or on the computer, changing size and style. 2. Write letters that make the **r**-controlled sound in a word two ways *(factory—factery)*. Choose the word that looks right—chances are it's correct.

1. Use strategy 1 to practise spelling the words on your list. Next, try to spell your words as a classmate dictates them to you. Use strategy 2 if you are uncertain about a particular spelling. Explain whether these strategies helped you learn to spell the words.

2. **Schwa vowels** are vowels that occur in unstressed syllables (see Unit 8). **R-controlled vowels** can occur in both stressed and unstressed syllables. Say each of your list words aloud. Write the syllables you hear. Mark the syllable you stress with a stress mark (′). Use a dictionary to check your completed work.

3. Find the **Words to Watch For** that complete these analogies. Write them in your notebook.

    a) *Carefree* is to *careless* what *worried* is to _____.
    b) *Thoughtful* is to *considerate* what *empathetic* is to _____.
    c) *Refined* is to *fragile* what *coarse* is to _____.
    d) *Rapid* is to *slow* what *different* is to _____.

4. As a class, make a version of **Words to Watch For** that includes words that many of you find difficult to spell. As you add words, try to organize them so that words with the same or similar difficult patterns are grouped together. Post your class list so that everyone can use it when they write.

Scroll Back

Edit and proofread your comparison, paying particular attention to the following checklist:

❏ Have you avoided using sentence fragments unintentionally?
❏ Have you used apostrophes for contractions and possessives?
❏ Have you avoided using apostrophes where only a plural is necessary?
❏ Are all words spelled correctly, including those containing **r**-controlled vowels?

Unit (11) Definition

What is a definition?

A definition is a description of a term that differentiates it from any other term. A definition may be as brief as a single word, or it can run for several pages. Here is a definition by Sylvia Funston entitled "Welcome to ESP!"

There are many reports of someone seeing a ghost of a friend or relative only to discover later that the person they saw died at the exact same time. Some scientists think that this is just a hallucination, a vision created in the brain of the person who "sees" the apparition, remembered later as coinciding with the loved one's death. Other people suggest that telepathy, or mind-to-mind communication, might be involved. The idea is that one person projects a telepathic image, which is received by someone else, who then "sees" the sender or "gets a message" from the sender. How it all happens is a mystery, but it definitely beats e-mail.

In case you hadn't sensed it, you're entering the world of extrasensory perception (ESP) where people supposedly can obtain information through some kind of sense beyond the ones we use to see, hear, touch, smell, taste, and know where our bodies are in space.

NAME

NON

No.

ESP/PARANORMAL

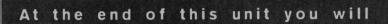

At the end of this unit you will

Know

- the features of a definition
- the difference between transitive and intransitive verbs, and direct and indirect objects
- when to use *which* or *that*
- that the roots of many words in the English language come from other languages

Be Able To

- write a definition
- distinguish between essential and nonessential clauses and phrases
- correctly punctuate nonessential clauses and phrases
- recognize some common Greek and Latin roots

ESP covers several strange talents in addition to telepathy: psychokinesis (the ability to use mind power to affect objects); precognition (seeing into the future); clairvoyance (the ability to see things happening over a great distance); clairaudience and clairsentience (the ability to hear and feel things happening far away). Parapsychologists have been testing ESP in laboratories since 1930, but except for one or two notable findings, they have so far failed to prove that ESP exists.

Checkpoint: Definition

Discuss how these characteristics of a definition apply to the model. Later, you can use the list to help you revise your own work.

✓ It usually begins with a general description of the item or idea. It may then list examples, features, or other details that make the description more specific.

✓ The amount of detail given, the examples chosen, and the language used is geared to the needs of the audience.

1. Write the following headings in your notebook. With a partner, list some concepts below each heading that interest you or that you recall having learned about. Some examples are given to help get you started.

Science	Social Studies	Language Arts	Math	Other
UFO	glacier	conflict	algebra	fashion
comet	earthquake	drama	geometry	music
electricity	apartheid	urban legend	probability	fear

2. Choose the concept that interests you most and that you think you could describe to a student one grade below you. Try writing a one-sentence definition of the concept that such a reader would understand.

3. Create a web of features, examples, or other details that you associate with the concept. (You may want to check encyclopedias, CD-ROMs, or a textbook to add to your information.) Complete your definition by adding information from your web that will help your audience understand the concept.

4. Refer back to the Checkpoint and revise your definition until you are satisfied with its focus, content, and organization.

GRAMMAR

Know
· the difference
between
transitive and
intransitive
verbs, and direct
and indirect
objects

Verbs that express action are either **transitive** or **intransitive**.

A **transitive verb** needs a noun phrase to complete its meaning. The noun phrase that completes a transitive verb is called a **direct object**.

Transitive Verb	Direct Object
One person **projects**	a telepathic image.
I **saw**	a ghost.
ESP **covers**	several strange talents.

Note that the thoughts expressed in the first column above do not make sense without the direct objects in the second column.

An **intransitive verb** can be modified, but it does not need a direct object.

Intransitive Verb	Modifier
The person **died**	at the same time.
The message **arrived**	telepathically.
The hoax **was uncovered**	when Dr. Who confessed.

This time, note that each of the thoughts expressed in the first column *could* stand alone as complete sentences. The modifiers in the second column add information, but they are not essential.

I. Indicate which of the following verbs are used transitively in the model and identify their direct objects.

think   sensed   beats   obtain   failed

A Challenge

Some verbs can be transitive or intransitive, depending on the context in which they are used. For example, consider the sentence *Dr. Jekyll ran the class after Mr. Hyde ran out of the room.* The first *ran* is transitive, while the second is intransitive. Working in teams or on your own, think up at least three more sentences using a single verb both transitively and intransitively.

Unit **11** Definition

Some transitive verbs—like *tell, send, give, ask,* and *show*—can have *two* objects: a **direct object** and an **indirect object.**

> A **direct object** answers *who* or *what* about a transitive verb; an **indirect object** answers *to whom, for whom, to what,* or *for what* about a transitive verb.

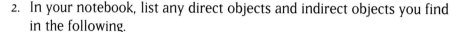

to whom?   what?
Erica's uncle gave <u>her</u>   <u>a laboratory kit</u>.
                indirect object   direct object

2. In your notebook, list any direct objects and indirect objects you find in the following.

   Dilip insists on definitions. For example, if I remark that a movie is brilliant, he challenges me to "define brilliant." But one night we saw a movie that terrified me. When we left the theatre, Dilip asked, "What did you think?" I shot him a sideways glance. He stared wildly back. Rain pelted us; the wind tossed us soggy newspapers. "Brilliant," I said finally. "Yeah," he replied.

3. Think of a way to illustrate graphically the relationships between the parts of the following sentences (for example, use a web, or a chart, etc.). Include the following information: subject, verb (transitive or intransitive), direct object, indirect object, and modifiers.

   My friend Sachiko bought her new dog a tree-sensing collar.

Language Link

MECHANICS

Be Able To
- distinguish between essential and nonessential clauses and phrases
- correctly punctuate nonessential clauses and phrases

Writing good definitions requires accuracy. To avoid misleading statements in your definitions (and in your writing generally), it is useful to know the difference between essential and nonessential phrases and clauses. A phrase or clause is essential if removing it changes the meaning of the sentence. Nonessential phrases or clauses give additional information, but the sentence can stand alone without them.

> Use **commas** to separate **nonessential clauses or phrases** from the rest of the sentence. *Never* use commas to separate **essential clauses or phrases** from the rest of the sentence.

Notice how the switch from essential to nonessential clause changes the meaning in the sentences below:

essential clause
Walruses are seals <u>that have large tusks</u>.

nonessential clause
Walruses are seals, <u>which have large tusks</u>.

1. State whether the subordinate clause in each sentence is essential (E) or nonessential (N). Then copy the sentence and add any necessary punctuation.

    a) Cars that run on mind power are much less polluting.
    b) *Popular Science* which I buy every month provides information about interesting inventions.
    c) Alysia's mother whom everyone calls Clair Voyant drives a taxi.

Subordinate clauses are discussed in Unit 9.

Strategy

Essential and nonessential phrases or clauses allow you to include information within one sentence, rather than writing two shorter sentences that can sound choppy.

2. Rewrite each of the following pairs of sentences as one sentence using a subordinate clause. Be sure to punctuate the new sentence correctly.

    a) Karl is performing in the school production of *Hamlet: A Ghost Story*. Karl is a talented actor.
    b) The man waited by the telephone booth. The man's feet did not appear to be touching the ground.
    c) Leigh bought Stephen King's latest novel. The novel is being made into a movie.

3. Look over your definition and make sure that essential and nonessential clauses are punctuated correctly.

Writing

USAGE & STYLE

Language
Link

Use **that** in essential clauses; use **which** in nonessential clauses.

Know

- when to use *which* or *that*

Unit 11 Definition

It is common to see *which* used for both essential and nonessential clauses. However, to help your reader differentiate the two, it helps to use *which* exclusively for the latter. (*That* always indicates an essential clause.)

> The idea is that one person projects a telepathic image, **which** is received by someone else.

1. Choose the correct word from inside the parentheses to complete the following sentences.

    a) The show *(that, which)* Monique saw made her curious about ESP.
    b) The show, *(that, which)* aired last night, lasted for two hours.
    c) Robertson Davies wrote *Murther and Walking Spirits, (that, which)* could be considered a ghost story.
    d) The Davies novel *(that, which)* I enjoyed most is *Fifth Business*.

2. Check your definition to make sure you have used *that* and *which* correctly.

Language
Link

SPELLING

Know
- that the roots of many words in the English language come from other languages

Be Able To
- recognize some common Greek and Latin roots

The English language began to develop in the fifth century A.D. in what is now Great Britain. It was a blend of German dialects, Celtic languages, and Latin. Later, it was combined with Norman French, which contained many Greek and Latin words.

 Words to Watch For

These words, taken from the definition at the beginning of the unit, were formed using roots from other languages.

scientist	vision	laboratories	communication	remembered
hallucination	sensory	psychologists	perception	notable

In your notebook, make a list of 8-10 words that contain a root from another language and that can be difficult to spell. You can use words from this box, the definition, or your personal reading. Use a dictionary to confirm the origin of the roots.

1. In a dictionary look up the histories of the **Words to Watch For**. Underline the root in each word (for example, *scientist* comes from the Latin word *scientia*, so its root is *scientist*).

Strategy

Choose two words from your word list. For each word, make a web of words that share the same root (write the root in the middle). List as many words as you can. When you finish, trade webs with a partner. Add any other related words to your partner's web.

2. Record the language of the root of each of the two words you chose. Now, find two words that come from other languages. Write these words, and their history, in your notebook.

3. Choose five **Words to Watch For**, and list the school subject where you would be most likely to use each one. Then include the word in a sentence that you might write in each subject.

4. Working in a group, find 10 examples of words we use today that come from a First Nations language. (Hint: Brainstorm words you know related to First Nations customs and culture, then check a dictionary to confirm their origin.) Tell what each word means, which First Nations people used the word, and the area the people inhabited.

5. Etymology means the origin and development of a language—its history. Become etymologists by making a class chart of words whose roots are from other languages. Keep adding words to the chart as you find them.

Scroll Back

Edit and proofread your definition, paying particular attention to the following.

❏ Have you used commas to set off nonessential clauses from the rest of the sentence?
❏ Have you used subordinate clauses to avoid short, choppy sentences?
❏ Have you used *which* and *that* correctly?
❏ Have you spelled all words correctly?

Unit **11** Definition

Unit 12 Hard News Story

What is a hard news story?

The term "hard news" is given to stories written about events that are happening now. While newspapers contain many different types of writing, including human interest stories, feature articles, columns, editorials, and letters, many readers feel that the most important writing in a newspaper is the hard news story.

Human Error Creates "Serious Trouble" on Mir

MOSCOW (AP) — The embattled Mir space station lost virtually all power Thursday when the crew accidentally disconnected a vital cable, but the three-man team was not in immediate danger, a top Russian space official said.

"Today we had a very bad situation, serious trouble," mission control chief Vladimir Solovyov told a news conference. "We have lost all energy." But he stressed that the crew was safe and was working to restore power in the Mir, which has been plagued by accidents and serious malfunctions in recent months.

Solovyov said the crew was making routine preparations to repair the Mir's already damaged power system Thursday when they accidentally disconnected a cable supplying power to the orientation system, which directs the solar panels to the sun.

At the end of this unit you will

Know

- the features of a hard news story
- when to use either the active or passive voice
- how parentheses and square brackets are used
- some rules involving double consonants
- whether to double the final consonant in a root word when adding a suffix

Be Able To

- write a hard news story
- change the passive to the active voice
- combine sentences using parentheses
- avoid overuse of parentheses
- add information to direct quotations by using square brackets
- rearrange elements of a sentence to avoid dangling modifiers

Solovyov said the Mir was twisting chaotically and its solar panels were not oriented toward the sun, but some energy was still reaching them. The error led to virtually a complete power cut in all systems—electricity, orientation, life support, and communications, Solovyov said.

"It was a human error, but everyone can make a mistake and we should not judge the crew too harshly," he added.

However, the crew can communicate with Mission Control from the Soyuz escape capsule, which has systems independent from the rest of the Mir. Asked if space officials are considering an evacuation, Solovyov said, "We have not approached this stage yet."

The Russian official said the U.S. space agency NASA was "rendering us very effective help." NASA is providing "all possible means of communications to ensure the communication with the station," Solovyov said. That includes switching on NASA's ground stations so the Mir can communicate with Russian or American space officials at all times. Normally, the Russians can only communicate for a few minutes out of every hour as the space station passes over Russian territory, 400 kilometres (250 miles) above the Earth.

WRITER'S WORKSHOP

Checkpoint: Hard News Story

Discuss how these characteristics of a hard news story apply to the model. Later, you can use the list to help you revise your own work.

- ✓ The first paragraph (called *the lead*) answers the questions who, what, when, where, why, and how.

- ✓ The remaining paragraphs fill in the background, from most important to least important.

- ✓ News stories stick to the facts; if opinions are included, they are presented as quotations (direct or indirect), and are often balanced by quotations expressing an opposing point of view.

- ✓ Paragraphs tend to be short (some are only one sentence), to make it easier to cut information from the story at press time.

1. As a class, brainstorm ideas for news stories centred around your school or community. (These could be school activities, sports competitions, community events, etc.) In small groups or on your own, choose one event to write a story about for a school newspaper.

2. Begin by collecting answers to the 5 W's + H: who, what, when, where, why, and how. Make sure your facts are accurate. If possible, interview at least one person who was involved in the event.

3. Use the information you have collected to write two or three leads (opening paragraphs) for your story, including the answers to the 5 W's. Choose the best lead, and then write the rest of your story. Make sure to keep your paragraphs short, and to include the most important information first.

4. Refer back to the Checkpoint and revise your story until you are satisfied with its focus, content, and organization.

GRAMMAR

In the **active voice**, the subject *performs* an action. In the **passive voice**, the subject *receives* an action.

Only transitive verbs can be expressed in the passive voice.

> **Passive voice:** The space station was hit by a meteor.
> **Active voice:** A meteor hit the space station.

A Challenge

Describe what happens to the elements of the sentence above when it is changed from the passive to the active voice. Prepare a chart like this one to present your findings to the class.

	Subject	Verb Form	Direct Object
Passive Voice			
Active Voice			

Most writers avoid the passive voice because it is less direct and uses more words than necessary.

I. The following sentences are written in passive voice. Rewrite them in active voice. (You will have to include the person, or people, who you think might perform the action.) Use as few words as possible to say the same thing.

   a)   The astronauts were contacted every hour.
   b)   Detailed notes are recorded at every NASA meeting.
   c)   Repairs to the solar panels were carried out yesterday.

Although most writers prefer to use the active voice, there are some situations where the passive voice is useful.

Use the passive voice when the doer of the action is unimportant or unknown.

The repair mission was delayed twice.
Comets have been recorded as early as 240 B.C.

Know
- when to use either the active or passive voice

Be Able To
- change the passive to the active voice

See Unit 11 for transitive and intransitive verbs.

Unit **12** Hard News Story

2. Look through some news stories in your local paper and find an example of the passive voice. Copy or paste the example in your notebook and explain whether you think the writer had a good reason to use the passive voice instead of the active voice.

3. Look over your hard news article and see if you can find examples of sentences written in the passive voice. If you do not have a good reason for using the passive voice, rewrite them in the active voice.

MECHANICS

Know

- how parentheses and square brackets are used

Be Able To

- combine sentences using parentheses
- avoid overuse of parentheses
- add information to direct quotations by using square brackets

Use **parentheses** ( ) for material that supplements the information in the sentence, or for short asides or afterthoughts.

Normally, the Russians can only communicate for a few minutes... as the space station passes over Russian territory, 400 kilometres (250 miles) above the Earth.

The repair mission (which has already been delayed twice) is currently planned for the night of July 24–25.

1. In your notebook, rewrite each of the following pairs as one sentence. Use parentheses to insert the second sentence into the first. (Try to use as few words as possible within the parentheses. This will help to make your writing more direct, in the style of a hard news story.)

    a) The Mir has been plagued with malfunctions. The Mir is a Russian space station.
    b) The crew's best chance for survival was the escape capsule. Actually, the escape capsule was their *only* chance for survival.
    c) The solar panels were facing the wrong way. They are still facing the wrong way.

2. Read through your hard news story and evaluate your use of parentheses. Then look back at some other writing you have completed recently. Do you tend to overuse parentheses? How else could you incorporate the information?

Use **square brackets** [ ] to enclose words that you have added to a direct quotation.

News reporters often use brackets to add necessary information to direct quotations. In this way they use as few words as possible to make the quotation understandable to the reader.

Original quotation:	"We found four stolen television sets in Julian's car."
Adapted version:	Police Chief Ivan Bernowski told reporters, "We found four stolen television sets in [suspect René] Julian's car."
Original quotation:	"I won it for my supporting role in *All Flags Waving*."
Adapted version:	"I won [the Academy Award] for my supporting role in *All Flags Waving*," explained Sarmazian.

3. Look at any quotations that you may have included in your hard news story. Could you use square brackets to add necessary information, instead of having to include the information in a separate sentence? Rewrite these quotations using square brackets.

USAGE & STYLE

Language Link

A modifier is said to **dangle** when it is not clear what word it modifies.

To correct a dangling modifier, you can either insert the word being modified immediately before or after the dangling phrase, or change the phrase to a subordinate clause, with its own subject and predicate.

Be Able To
· rearrange elements of a sentence to avoid dangling modifiers

Problem: Having accidentally disconnected a vital cable, the space station lost all power Thursday.

insert the word being modified
Solution: The crew having accidentally disconnected a vital cable, the space station lost all power Thursday.

change the phrase to a subordinate clause
Solution: Because the crew accidentally disconnected a vital cable, the space station lost all power Thursday.

Unit **12** Hard News Story

1. Rewrite the following sentences, making changes that will correct the dangling modifiers.

   a) Racing against time, the fire on board the space station was extinguished before it could cause serious damage.
   b) Powerless to help, the crew could not rely on Mission Control during the crisis.
   c) Practically bankrupt, cosmonauts in the Russian space program get paid a fraction of what American astronauts receive.
   d) The international space station is being built by many nations in orbit.

A Challenge

Think up funny one-liners that use dangling modifiers. Here's one to get you started. (It's from the movie *Animal Crackers*, which starred the famous Marx Brothers comedy team.)

"One morning I shot an elephant in my pyjamas. How he got in my pyjamas, I'll never know."

Working with a partner, perform your one-liners in front of the class.

SPELLING

Know
- some rules involving double consonants
- whether to double the final consonant in a root word when adding a suffix

Which spellings would you choose: **ocasion** or **occasion**? **Prefered** or **preferred**? **Beginning** or **begining**? It can be tricky to know when double consonants are required, especially when you are adding a suffix to a word that ends with a consonant. Fortunately, there are some rules that can help. (But remember that there are exceptions to every rule!)

1. In one-syllable words that have a consonant-vowel-consonant pattern, double the final consonant when adding a suffix (*pet—petted; drum—drumming*).

2. In words with more than one syllable, double consonants follow a short vowel sound (*attempt, assign*).

3. In words that end in an **le** pattern, double consonants come before the **le** pattern when the vowel sound is short (*battle, scuffle*).

4. In multi-syllable words, where the stress is placed on the last syllable, double the final consonant when adding a suffix (*refer—referred*). An exception to this rule is a word like *support (supported)*.

Words to Watch For

These words, taken from the news story at the beginning of the unit, contain double consonants.

embattled	accidentally	immediate	normally	mission
virtually	disconnected	approached	batteries	planned

In your notebook, make a list of 8-10 words that contain at least one set of double consonants and that can be difficult to spell. You can use words from this box, the news story, and your personal reading. To help you learn the words, underline the double consonants in each word.

1. Reread the rules outlined at the beginning of the spelling unit, then look at your word list. Beside each word, write the number of the rule that applies.

2. Work with a partner. Write three words that apply to each rule. You can use the words from your list.

3. In your notebook, write the **Words to Watch For** that could be included in each set.

   a) most, nearly all, _____   b) right away, now, _____

   c) usually, typically, _____   d) thought out, intended, arranged, _____

4. In groups, brainstorm some exceptions to the rules above. Compare your words with those of the class.

5. Read the final rule. Now, write a rule that applies to adding suffixes to words where the stress is on initial syllables.

Scroll Back

Edit and proofread your news story, paying particular attention to the following checklist:

❏ Have you used the active voice whenever possible, and the passive voice only when it's justified?

❏ Have you used parentheses only when necessary?

❏ Have you used square brackets to add necessary information to direct quotations?

❏ Have you inserted all modifying phrases as close as possible to the word they modify, to avoid dangling modifiers?

❏ Are all words spelled correctly, including those that require double consonants?

Unit 12 Hard News Story

Persuasion

Persuasive writing is writing that gets things done—that moves readers to believe or to act. Whether you're trying to persuade government officials to clean up an environmental hazard or simply to convince a friend that one James Bond film is superior to all other James Bond films, persuasive writing is an effective means of presenting and defending a position and encouraging readers to support it as well.

This section contains four forms of persuasive writing: review, letter to the editor, editorial, and résumé and covering letter (which we treat together). By anticipating the viewpoints of their readers and carefully organizing details that support their purposes, the authors of these pieces demonstrate how to use writing to achieve a variety of goals.

Features of Persuasion

- Persuasive writing aims to move the reader to support a point of view or to act in support of an idea or cause.

- A persuasive piece often begins with a statement of the author's position, then presents arguments and evidence in favour of that position, and concludes with a call to action or a recommendation.

- Persuasive writers arrange their points in a way that best suits their argument.

- Although persuasion may involve appeals to emotion, the most effective arguments are usually backed up by facts and logical arguments.

Unit (13) Review

What is a review?

A review has two main purposes: it announces that a book, film, recording, or event is available to the public, and it helps people decide whether or not to read, view, buy, or attend. Besides having these purposes, however, reviews are usually entertaining to read.

12

This Bat Doesn't Fly by Jay Stone

WELL, THEY'VE SURE TAKEN THE BATMAN movies about as far as they can go. In today's Hollywood, that means over the edge into that hyperfast, hyperexpensive zone of pure, dizzying overkill.

What started four movies ago as a dark, comic-strip version of a Gothic city where surreal villains battled a troubled superhero has been turned, in *Batman & Robin*, into a cavalcade of special effects silliness, a non-story buried under too much money and too many gimmicks and too many villains battling too many superheroes. No one is troubled any more, except perhaps the poor moviegoer.

Batman & Robin is a strain to sit through. The comic that became a myth has been turned back into a comic, a bad one this time.

It's not just the lack of story and the lousy characters and the acting that ranges from pedestrian (Arnold Schwarzenegger as the villain Freeze) to the excruciating (Uma Thurman as the villain Poison Ivy, the worst performance by a major star this year). It's also that *Batman & Robin* isn't any fun.

Not that it doesn't try. You can practically see the stretch marks on this baby. *Batman & Robin* is directed by Joel Schumacher, whose *Batman Forever*, the third in the series, was a portent of the endless-action mishmash that he has accomplished here. This movie seems to be based on the theory that if one hero is good and two heroes are twice as good, then maybe three heroes will be thousands of times as good. If one cliffhanger is exciting, ten of them (all shot with the same movie-video, edited-in-a-food-processor style) will be sensational. If it's funny to call the heroes

Know

- the features of a review
- when to write numbers as numerals, and when to spell them out
- the difference between *accept* and *except*
- some basic prefixes

Be Able To

- write a review
- avoid some common errors in subject-verb agreement
- add prefixes to words

"the bat and the bird," then let's say it fifty times and it will be hilarious.

The story, as written by Akiva Goldsman, the co-writer of *Batman Forever* and collaborator with Schumacher on a couple of John Grisham movies, is barely legible. Freeze, the new supervillain, has been terrorizing the city by shooting his freeze-them gun at everything and stealing diamonds, the "ice" that keeps him going until he can discover the cure for his wife's illness and thaw her from her cryogenic state (Freeze was a chemist and Olympic athlete before becoming a supervillain).

Thurman plays Poison Ivy, a kind of mad ecologist with deadly lips and a supply of secret powder that makes men fall in love with her. Thurman doesn't appear to know what to make of this character either, so she plays it like a sort of thin Mae West in a green bodysuit. Every time she takes out the love powder, a soprano saxophone wails and so did I. Poison Ivy travels with a third villain, a sort of assistant named Bane, who is pumped up like early Schwarzenegger. They use him to open doors.

On the other side of the ledger is Robin (the game Chris O'Donnell) who is all grown up now and wants his own Bat signal and an identity separate from that of Batman. Joining them is the amateurish Alicia Silverstone, who becomes Batgirl about twenty minutes from the end of the picture but before that is a visiting scholar from England who is adept at judo and learned to ride a motorcycle to get over the tragic death of both her parents.

This film shows what happens when films are taken away from directors with a vision, such as Tim Burton had when he created the world of the first *Batman*, and given to the packagers. They then get together to decide just what it is that is selling their films. Is it the costumes maybe, or the villains with their professional wrestling-type "themes"? Is it the bat-shaped gizmos?

Whatever. Let's throw them all in. It is up to the public to throw them all out.

WRITER'S WORKSHOP

Checkpoint: Review

Discuss how these characteristics of a review apply to the model. Later, you can use the list to help you revise your own work.

✓ Its purposes are to *inform* (providing a partial plot summary, without revealing the ending); *persuade* (supporting an opinion with examples); and *entertain* (through humour, interesting comparisons, or choice of language).

✓ A film review focuses on plot, characters, acting, directing, cinematography (angles, lighting, etc.), and script.

✓ A book review focuses on plot, characterization, writing style, and diction.

1. In your notebook, make a list of all the books you have read and/or films you have seen in the last two months. Put a check mark beside the ones you feel most strongly about—either positively or negatively. Choose ONE of these that you remember most clearly and decide whether you will recommend this book or film to others.

2. Briefly describe the plot of the book or film without giving away too much of the story.

3. Make two columns in your notebook. In one, list all the things you liked about the book or film. In the other, identify the things you disliked. Be as specific as possible, and back up each point with an example. (Your review will be more convincing if you identify both strengths and weaknesses, so try to find some of each.)

4. If you have read other books by the same author or seen films with the same star, identify specific ways in which this book/film is more or less effective than the others.

5. Decide the best order in which to present your ideas, and write a first draft.

6. Refer back to the Checkpoint and revise your review until you are satisfied with its focus, content, and organization.

GRAMMAR

Be Able To
- avoid some common errors in subject-verb agreement

A verb must **agree** in number with its subject.

You will usually do this automatically. However, you are more likely to make a mistake in subject-verb agreement

- when other words come between the subject and the verb
- when the subject is compound (made up of two or more nouns or pronouns joined by *and*)
- with words that look plural but are treated as singular

The noun in a **prepositional phrase** is never the subject of a sentence.

singular subject   prepositional phrase   singular verb

The Batman   in the old television shows   makes me laugh.

singular subject   prepositional phrases

One   of my favourite characters   from the old Batman series
is King Tut.
singular verb

Subjects joined by **and** always take a plural verb, *unless* they form a single unit.

plural subject   plural verb

Batman and Robin have become mythic figures in North America.

singular subject   singular verb

The fish and chips at the concession stand was more satisfying
than the red herrings served up in this movie.

If the subject contains two words joined by **or** or **nor,** make the verb agree with the part of the subject that is nearest to it.

plural subject   plural verb

Neither Poison Ivy nor the other villains   are a match for the
dynamic duo, of course.

Unit **13** Review

Most **indefinite pronouns** are treated as singular. However, **all, any,** and **some** may be singular or plural depending on the noun or pronoun they refer to.

Indefinite pronouns include *each, every, none, everyone, everybody, everything, someone, somebody, anyone, anybody, neither,* and *no one.*

singular subject   singular verb

<u>Most</u> of the film   <u>is</u> dull.

plural subject   plural verb

<u>Most</u> of the characters <u>are</u> cartoonish.

Words like **mathematics, economics, news,** and **statistics** look plural, but take a singular verb.

singular verb

News of the caped crusader <u>spread</u> throughout the city.

1. Rewrite these sentences, correcting any errors in subject-verb agreement.

   a) Each of the films feature a different plot, but the portrayal of the characters are the same throughout.
   b) The film version of *The Sound and the Hurry* are a lot better than the book.
   c) Neither the plot nor the characters makes *As I Lay Crying* a worthwhile film.

2. Look back over your review and correct any errors in subject-verb agreement.

Language Link

MECHANICS

Know

· when to write numbers as numerals, and when to spell them out

As a rule of thumb, spell out round numbers and numbers from one to nine; otherwise, use numerals.

If one hero is good and two heroes are twice as good, then maybe three heroes will be thousands of times as good.

I know someone who has seen this film 17 times.

126

However, this varies depending on the level and style of writing.

- Very informal writing and scientific writing often use numerals for all numbers.
- Very formal writing may spell out everything from one to infinity.

No matter what kind of writing you are doing, it is important to **be consistent** in your use of numbers.

> Regardless of the numerical style you adopt, always spell out numbers at the beginning of a sentence. In addition, it is usually acceptable to use numerals to express the following:
>
> | percentages | dates | addresses | time |
> | temperatures | page numbers | exact amounts of money | |

1. In small groups, look through a science textbook, newspaper, and encyclopedia, and analyze the numerical style used in each. How are they the same? How do they differ? What accounts for the differences? How is the style appropriate to the text? Record your findings in a chart or diagram and present them to the class.

2. Check that you have used a consistent numerical style in your review as well as in three other pieces of writing you have completed recently.

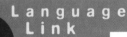

USAGE & STYLE

Language Link

Know

- the difference between *accept* and *except*

> **Accept** is a verb, meaning "to receive." **Except** is a preposition, meaning "excluding."

The actor refused to **accept** the Academy Award.

No one is troubled any more, **except** perhaps the poor moviegoer.

1. Choose the correct word from inside the parentheses.

   a) I have enjoyed every film made by this director—*(accept, except)* this one.

   b) I just could not *(accept, except)* the choice of actors in this remake.

   c) In her *(acceptance, exceptance)* speech, she thanked everyone *(accept, except)* her third cousin.

Unit **13** Review

2. Make a list of other words that create usage problems for writers. Use each word correctly in a sentence, and invent a way to help you remember how to use the words correctly.

SPELLING

Know
- some basic prefixes

Be Able To
- add prefixes to words

A **prefix,** which is a word part added to the beginning of a word, can change the word's meaning in a number of ways. Here are some examples.

- **un-, dis-,** or **non-** can make a word mean the opposite (*happy—unhappy; appear—disappear; sense—nonsense*)
- **inter-** can make a word mean between or among something (*lock—interlock*)
- **extra-** can make a word mean outside or beyond something (*curricular—extracurricular*)
- **hyper-** can make a word mean above or beyond something (*active—hyperactive*)

This lesson will focus on prefixes and how they are added to words.

Words to Watch For

Some of these words have been taken from the movie review at the beginning of the unit. Others share a root with words in the review or have been added to represent words you may need to learn. All contain a prefix.

excruciating	surreal	discover	unaccomplished	nonsense
hyperfast	ecologist	trilogy	unexciting	illogical

In your notebook, list 8-10 words that have a prefix and that can be difficult to spell. You can use words from the box, the movie review, and your personal reading. To help you learn the words, underline the prefix in each word. Some will be easier (like the prefixes **non-, dis-,** and **un-**), while others will be harder (like the prefixes **ex-** and **eco-**).

1. Fill in the missing letters to complete these **Words to Watch For**. Write them in your notebook.

a) _ _ _ _ _ _ _ e   b) _ _ s _ _ _ _ _   c) _ _ c _ _ _ _ _ _ _ _
d) _ _ _ l _ _ _

Strategy

Completing missing letter puzzles like those in question 1 can help you spell a word. Give your word list to a partner. She or he can use it to make missing letter puzzles. Do the same for your partner. When finished, trade pages to complete your lesson words.

2. Look at the prefix you underlined in each word in your list. Write how each prefix changes the meaning of the word to which it is added.

3. The three Batman movies that came before the one reviewed could be called a *trilogy*. In your notebook write why this is so, then write three other words that begin with the prefix **tri-**.

4. In the review the writer used the word *non-story*. How would you define *non-story?* Write your definition in your notebook.

5. We often use *hyper* as a a short form for the word *hyperactive*. What prefix has the opposite meaning of **hyper-**?

6. With a partner, brainstorm three prefixes that have not been mentioned in this section. Come up with a list of five words that begin with each of the prefixes. Then state what the prefixes mean.

Scroll Back

Edit and proofread your review, paying particular attention to the following checklist:

❏ Do all your verbs agree in number with their subject?
❏ Have you used a style of writing numbers that is both consistent and appropriate to the level of language?
❏ Have you used *accept/except*, or any other confusing word pairs, correctly?
❏ Have you spelled all words correctly, especially those that contain prefixes?

Unit **13** Review

Unit ⑭ Letter to the Editor

What is a letter to the editor?

Most newspapers and magazines include an opinion page, where individuals can submit letters to the editor expressing their views on various issues. A letter to the editor is a good way to get your voice heard!

Don't Tell Us What to Wear

This letter addresses all the moms and dads who can't stand what their children wear.

I'm sixteen years old and recently my mother threw out my two favourite pairs of jeans, the reason being they both had holes. One had a small hole in the back showing some bare skin (or my bum, as my parents claim). The other had a hole in the knee. The anger that surged through my body cannot be described in words. I went so crazy, I had this urge to cut my mom's clothes with scissors. Then I came very close to leaving my house and going to a friend's house. However, I didn't follow through.

My mother thinks wearing ripped jeans (or baggy clothes, for that matter) reflects on my personality, not to mention on the family. She worries people will be gossiping. I don't care what people say because people talk, regardless of what you wear. Most parents grew up in a very different time, when dressing up in nice clothes said everything about you. I like to think we have become more modern and do not judge people by appearances.

My anguish comes from all the suffering something so irrelevant has ignited. When I read about the problems parents have with kids, ranging from taking drugs, misbehaving, to getting pregnant and quitting school, I think my mother should count her blessings.

Moms and dads, this is a vital stage in an adolescent's life. Teens are going through many changes, trying to find themselves. Forcing them to be a mirror image of you restricts them from developing into their own persons. Imposing your power by telling us what to wear takes a piece of our identity away.

So, unless your child wears a lobster suit to school, relax.

—Tina G.

Know

- the features of a letter to the editor
- the difference between a simple and a compound sentence
- effective uses of simple and compound sentences
- two ways that colons are used
- the difference between formal, informal, and nonstandard language
- how changes in syllable stress can affect vowel sound

Be Able To

- write your own letter to the editor
- use colons to make your writing more effective

Ride Bikes More Often

The number of people driving cars in Halifax has increased, and so has air pollution from car exhaust. One way we could solve this problem is by encouraging people to ride bicycles more often. We can do this in three ways:

1) Make room for bicycle lanes on a few roads. Select several roads running east/west and north/south that cars would not be able to park on so that both drivers and bicyclists are happy.
2) Teach bicyclists to ride safely and to respect cars.
3) Teach student drivers to be aware of bicyclists.

By doing this, we can make the air fresher to breathe and make Halifax a nicer place to live in.

—Elizabeth T.

WRITER'S WORKSHOP

Checkpoint: Letter to the Editor

Discuss how these characteristics of a letter to the editor apply to the models. Later, you can use the list to help you revise your own work.

✓ Its purpose may be to bring a topic to people's attention or to persuade people to take action on an issue.

✓ It should be brief and to the point.

✓ Arguments are arranged in an effective order. The introduction needs a strong argument to capture readers attention. The conclusion must contain an even stronger argument to make readers think about the issue after they have finished reading.

It often ends with a call to action, a question, or a summary of the main arguments.

1. In your notebook, make a chart with the following headings: SCHOOL ISSUES, COMMUNITY ISSUES, and GLOBAL ISSUES. Working with a partner, brainstorm at least five issues under each heading. Then decide which of these topics you feel strongest about.

Idea File

A school issue might be a policy that does not permit the wearing of hats in the building; a community issue might be the need for a recreational facility; and a global issue might be the need to protect the rain forests.

2. On a separate sheet of paper, write one sentence stating your opinion on the issue you have chosen, then list at least three reasons, examples, or facts to explain why you feel this way.

3. Arrange your notes in a logical order, and write a first draft of your letter. Be brief, but include enough information so that your reader understands what the issue is. Find a suitable conclusion for your letter.

4. Refer back to the Checkpoint and revise your letter until you are satisfied with its focus, content, and organization.

GRAMMAR

A **simple sentence** contains only one subject and one predicate.

A simple sentence is made up of one independent clause.

> subject   predicate
> The other had a hole in the knee.

Although a simple sentence has only one subject and one predicate, both the subject and the predicate can be compound.

> compound subject
> My mother *and* my father hate my clothes.

> compound predicate
> By doing this, we can make the air fresher to breathe *and* make Halifax a nicer place to live.

1. Find at least five simple sentences in "Don't Tell Us What to Wear," and copy these sentences in your notebook. Circle the subject and underline the predicate in each.

See Unit 5 for subjects and predicates, and Unit 9 for clauses.

A **compound sentence** is formed when two independent clauses are joined by a coordinating conjunction.

> independent clause   coordinating conjunction   independent clause
> I am sixteen years old   and   my mother recently threw out my two favourite pairs of jeans.

Strategy

To distinguish between a compound sentence and a simple sentence with a compound predicate, draw an imaginary line at the coordinating conjunction (*and, but, or, nor, for, yet, so*). If it is a compound sentence, each side will have its own subject and its own predicate. If it is a compound predicate, the second verb will not have a separate subject of its own.

Unit 14 Letter to the Editor

2. Decide if each of the following sentences is a simple or a compound sentence. Explain how you know.

   a) I came very close to leaving my house and going to a friend's house.

   b) The anger surged through my body, and I almost reached for the scissors.

   c) I need to become my own person, but my parents won't let me.

Strategy

Compound sentences can make your writing flow, but using a short, simple sentence is often a good way to emphasize a contrasting point. For example, *My mother thinks wearing ripped jeans reflects on my personality. I don't care.*

3. Look back at your letter to the editor and think about how you could use simple sentences to emphasize a point. Also think about combining simple sentences to make your writing flow more smoothly. Make any changes you think will improve your writing.

MECHANICS

Know
- two ways that colons are used

Use a **colon** after an independent clause to introduce a list or a quotation.

Be Able To
- use colons to make your writing more effective

One way we could solve this problem is by encouraging people to ride bicycles more often. We can do this in three ways: ...

1. Identify which of the following passages use colons correctly to introduce a list. Remember that the colon must come after an independent clause.

   a) Urban cyclists should make sure their bicycles have two extra pieces of equipment: a mirror to see traffic approaching from the rear, and a horn to warn pedestrians who might step into their path.

b) The most important features to look for in a bicycle helmet are: a hard plastic covering, secure straps, and sufficient ventilation.

c) To ensure their safety, cyclists should wear the following items: a helmet, reflective clothing, and knee and elbow pads.

> Use a colon to indicate that the phrase or clause that follows describes or is in some way related to what came before.

I want to raise an issue of great concern to students: year-round schooling.

Rain forests are the lungs of the Earth: they allow the planet to breathe.

2. What other punctuation marks could have been used in the two sentences above, instead of the colons? What effect does the colon have in each case?

3. Check through your letter to the editor to see if you have used any colons. If you have, make sure they are used correctly. If not, are there any places where a colon might make your writing more effective?

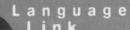

USAGE & STYLE

Know
- the difference between formal, informal, and nonstandard language

> The appropriate level of language to use when communicating depends on the writer's or speaker's audience and purpose.

There is no right or wrong language level—just language that is more appropriate or less appropriate for a particular context.

- **formal:** when writing to people you do not know well
- **informal:** when writing to friends or family
- **nonstandard:** when speaking or writing dialogue

1. Look at the examples of formal, informal, and nonstandard language on the next page. Working with a partner, make a list of characteristics you notice about each style. How would you characterize the style of the two letters at the beginning of this unit? Which is more formal? Why?

135

Formal Language

I wish to apply for the position of lifeguard at the community pool. You will note from the enclosed résumé that I have two years experience as a lifeguard as well as advanced Red Cross certification in life-saving training. I have excellent referees who will attest to my outstanding character and professionalism, and I would appreciate being granted an interview during which I can discuss my qualifications at greater length.

Informal Language

I'd like to apply for the job of lifeguard at the community pool. I've worked as a lifeguard for two years and I've completed the highest-level Red Cross life-saving course. My references will tell you that I'm well suited for the job. I'd like an interview with you so I can discuss further why I think I'm the best person for the job.

Nonstandard Language

Like, I wuz wonderin' if you wuz still needin' a lifeguard at yer pool. I done worked as a lifeguard fer two year, 'n' I done took the top Red Cross course fer life-savin'. I got three dudes who'll lay it on thick about me. Can we get together 'n' yap about it?

2. Rewrite the first three paragraphs of "Don't Tell Us What to Wear," first in a more formal style and then in nonstandard dialogue.

3. Tape yourself giving an oral presentation based on your letter to the editor (don't have the written version in front of you). Then transcribe the tape. How would you describe your spoken language? How does it differ from the written version of your letter?

Language Link

SPELLING

Know
- how changes in syllable stress can affect vowel sound

Say the word *invite*. Now add **-tion**—*invitation*—and listen to the changed sound of **i** in the second syllable. The word *invite* follows the vowel-consonant-silent **e** pattern. In many of these words, vowel sounds can change when the stress is placed on another syllable because of an added prefix or suffix. Words that follow this pattern are not the only words in which vowel sounds can change. In the word *major*, for example, the stress is placed on the first syllable. When you add the suffix **-ity**, the stress is placed on the second syllable. This makes the vowel sound change from a schwa to **r**-controlled. In this unit, we will look at words where vowel sounds change according to syllable stress.

Words to Watch For

Some of these words have been taken from the letters to the editor at the beginning of this unit. In all the words, a vowel sound can change when the syllable stress changes.

describe	ignite	relate	design	degrade
impose	explain	admire	provide	receive

In your notebook, make a list of 8-10 words in which a vowel sound can change when the syllable stress changes. You can use words from this box, the letters to the editor, and your personal reading.

1. Write each lesson word according to its syllable breaks. Mark the vowel sounds you hear: short *(bŭt)*, long *(tāke)*, schwa (abəl).

2. These words contain the roots of the **Words to Watch For**. In each word, however, a suffix has been added that changes the stressed syllable and a vowel sound. Write these words according to their syllable breaks. Mark the vowel sounds you hear. Circle the vowel sound that changed.

   a) relative   b) designation   c) degradation   d) description
   e) ignition   f) explanation   g) admiration   h) imposition

3. Change some **Words to Watch For** by following these directions. Write them in your notebook.

   a) *provide* to mean one who provides   b) *explain* to the past tense
   c) *describe* to a plural noun   d) *admire* to an adjective

4. The five vowels make many different vowel sounds. Working with a partner, identify as many vowel sounds as you can. (Remember that some vowel sounds are made when vowels work together or with the letters **r, w,** and **y.**) Find example words that show the different letter patterns that make each vowel sound you identified.

Scroll Back

Edit and proofread your letter to the editor, paying particular attention to the following checklist:

- ❏ Have you used simple sentences effectively?
- ❏ Have you used a variety of sentence structures?
- ❏ Have you used colons correctly?
- ❏ Have you used a level of language that is consistent and appropriate?
- ❏ Are all words spelled correctly?

Unit 14   **Letter to the Editor**

Unit 15 Editorial

What is an editorial?

A newspaper or magazine editorial is a short essay in which the writer presents his or her opinion about a current issue of concern. The following editorial appeared in *The Toronto Star*.

Ads in Our Schools

Reading, writing, and Reeboks? Commercial advertising is creeping into Ontario classrooms.

Students in Peel are confronted by ads for Trident gum and McDonald's on the computers they use for lessons. In York, students ride to schools on buses plastered with commercial messages. Reebok hasn't entered the fray yet, but Adidas has. It advertises inside the 800 school buses in York Region.

Trolling for advertising dollars is an understandable response by school boards that have lost hundreds of millions of dollars from their budgets in recent years. But trustees should remember it is their job to nurture independent thinking, not to deliver fresh minds to the marketplace.

Peel and York are stepping gingerly into the advertising market, consulting parents before launching pilot projects. Both say they have criteria to exclude offensive ads from school property.

Know

- the features of an editorial
- how to form a complex sentence
- two main uses of ellipses
- three principles of plain language
- some spelling patterns that suggest a Greek or Latin origin

Be Able To

- write an editorial
- identify three types of sentence structures
- use ellipses in excerpts from direct quotations
- apply some principles of plain language to your writing
- pluralize some words that have Greek or Latin endings

The products may not be out-and-out offensive, but they will appear to impressionable youngsters to have the blessing of school authorities. What is a Markham student to think about a teacher's nutrition lesson after riding to school on a bus that advertises a popular brand of candy?

But the problem is deeper than whether students will be influenced to buy something that might not be in their best interest. They should not be influenced to buy in school at all.

Society is saturated with messages designed to create artificial desire for goods. That's part of our consumer culture. But schools have been an oasis from all this rampant commercialism.

A big part of growing up and forging one's identity is to learn to distinguish your own tastes from those of others around you. Learning to buck the peer pressure of the schoolyard is difficult enough for students; they shouldn't have to struggle against the siren calls of commercials in the precincts of their schools as well.

Commercial advertising in schools is a growing American phenomenon. Canadian parents, teachers, students and trustees must join to stop the trend from creeping north. Otherwise, what's now a trickle of advertising in schools will turn into a flood.

WRITER'S WORKSHOP

Checkpoint: Editorial

Discuss how these characteristics of an editorial apply to the model. Later, you can use the list to help you revise your own work.

✓ Its subject is usually an issue of current concern.

✓ It often begins with a controversial question, an emotional appeal, or a catchy turn of phrase.

✓ It includes enough information to familiarize readers with the main facts surrounding an issue.

✓ It often includes arguments in favour of the other side of the debate, and then proves them wrong.

✓ Arguments are usually backed up with facts or examples.

1. You are the editor of your school newspaper, preparing to write an editorial on advertising in schools. List each of the arguments used in the model. Then write a counterargument for each, proving that advertising in schools is a positive thing.

2. Working with a partner, invent at least two other reasons why advertising would be a positive thing for the schools in your district.

3. Arrange your arguments in a logical order, and write an editorial that will catch your readers' interest and convince them of your position.

4. Refer back to the Checkpoint and revise your work until you are satisfied with its focus, content, and organization.

GRAMMAR

Know

- how to form a complex sentence

A **complex sentence** consists of an independent clause and one or more subordinate clauses.

Be Able To

- identify three types of sentence structures

independent clause   subordinate clause

What is a student to think about nutrition lessons when he or she rides to school on a bus advertising candy?

To add even more variety to your sentences, try reversing the order of the independent and subordinate clauses. (Always use a comma after a subordinate clause if it comes before the independent clause.)

Subordinate clauses are discussed in Unit 9.

independent clause   subordinate clause

Many people are against advertising in schools because it gives a bad impression.

subordinate clause   independent clause

Because it gives a bad impression, many people are against advertising in schools.

1. Indicate whether each of the following sentences is simple, compound, or complex. Explain how you know.

Simple and compound sentences are discussed in Unit 14.

a) The ads on the school bus at least give me something to look at!

b) Although schools profit from the ads, I don't want to read dumb slogans in class every day.

c) I see those ads everywhere, and I can't stand it anymore!

MECHANICS

Language Link

An **ellipsis** is the omission of one or more words from a direct quotation. An ellipsis is shown by three dots.

Know
- the two main uses of ellipses

Be Able To
- use ellipses in excerpts from direct quotations

1. Read the following passage and locate the part of the editorial it comes from. Working with a partner, discuss how this passage is different from the model. Identify as many differences as you can.

Peel and York ... have criteria to exclude offensive ads from school property.

Generally, you do not have to use ellipses at the beginning or the end of a quotation, unless you leave the last sentence unfinished. In that case, add a period to the ellipsis points.

Peel and York ... have criteria to exclude offensive ads....

Unit 15 Editorial

2. With a partner, brainstorm a list of reasons why a writer might want to omit words in a quotation.

3. Choose a different passage from the model and rewrite it using an ellipsis.

Never use ellipses to alter the original meaning of a quotation.

4. Compare the following quotations with the original passages in the model. Decide if the writer has used ellipses fairly. If your answer is no, explain why. If your answer is yes, correct any errors in the writer's use of ellipses.

   a) I agree with *The Toronto Star* that "Trustees should remember it is their job ... to deliver fresh minds to the marketplace...."

   b) In the editorial, the *Star* writes, "The products may not be ... offensive, but they will appear to have the blessing of school authorities."

   c) In a recent editorial, *The Toronto Star* stated that, "Commercial advertising in schools is a growing phenomenon...." Let's make sure our schools are part of this innovative trend!

Idea File

Besides showing that words have been omitted, the ellipsis has another function. It can be used when writing dialogue to indicate that a sentence is unfinished.

"Ah, you see," mumbled Jeff, looking at the floor, "I didn't ... I mean, I ... I wasn't expecting you to find out ... er ... I thought I could return it before you ... ah ... found out it was missing."

5. Look back through some of your writing that uses dialogue, and consider whether using ellipses might help make your writing more realistic.

USAGE & STYLE

When you write something formal like an editorial, don't confuse formal language with big words and complex sentence structures. The following principles of plain language should apply regardless of the level of language you are using.

Know
- three principles of plain language

Be Able To
- apply some principles of plain language to writing

Write the way you speak.

This does not mean imitating exactly what you would say if you were talking to a friend—writing is usually more formal and more grammatically correct than everyday speech. But it does mean that you should be able to read your writing aloud comfortably.

1. Try reading your editorial aloud. Are any words or phrases hard to read naturally? What changes can you make so that your own voice comes through?

Use simple words.

Complex: Prior to embarking upon an excursion of a lengthy duration, wayfarers employing two-wheeled conveyances customarily determine the most expeditious route.

Simple: Before a long trip, cyclists usually plan the most direct route.

2. Working with a partner, rewrite the following sentences using simpler words. Refer to a dictionary for the meanings of unfamiliar terms.

   a) The primary objective of an individual's accoutrement must be the sheathing of the epidermal layer in such a way as to prevent discomfort resulting from exposure to inclement atmospheric conditions.

   b) One should eschew the company of sycophants whose obsequious fawning, while ingratiating, is entirely ephemeral.

Unit 15 Editorial

> Make every word count.

Avoid the passive voice, because it uses more words. Avoid negative statements when a positive one will do. And avoid overly complicated formulations such as the following:

Instead of ...	Use ...
owing to the fact that	since/because
there is no doubt that	no doubt
it appears that	it seems
with regard to	about

3. Check through your editorial with the principles of plain language in mind. Can you improve the clarity of your writing?

Language Link

SPELLING

Know

- some spelling patterns that suggest a Greek or Latin origin

Be Able To

- pluralize some words that have Greek or Latin endings

Many words we use today, particularly in the areas of science and math, come from Greek and Latin. Unlike most English words, which are made plural by adding **-s** or **-es**, these words take irregular (at least for us) endings. In this unit, we will look at some common Greek and Latin word endings and how they are made plural.

Words to Watch For

All these words are of Greek or Latin origin. Some have been taken from the editorial at the beginning of the unit, while the others have been added to represent spelling patterns that are useful for you to recognize.

criterion	medium	basis	stimulus	memorandum
phenomenon	curriculum	analysis	oasis	crisis

In your notebook, list 8-10 words that have Greek or Latin origin. Use a dictionary that contains etymologies (word histories) to confirm your choices. You can use words from the box, the letters, and your personal reading.

1. Group your words according to their endings. Use these headings for your chart:

-on	-um	-is	-us

Strategy

A dictionary is a great source of information about words. In a senior dictionary, you will find each word's spelling, syllable breaks, phonetic spelling (for pronunciation), part of speech, meaning(s), and origin. Have a dictionary available to complete the following activities.

2. You may know the plural form of one or more of your words. Make the word plural, then add the same ending to the rest of the words in that column. Check your work in a dictionary, then make words in other columns plural using the same process.

3. The plural form of one of the **Words to Watch For** is often misused. Can you identify the word? Write two sentences—one showing the plural used incorrectly, and the other with the plural used correctly.

4. Write each of your words on a piece of paper. On another piece of paper, write its definition, and on a third piece, its history.

criterion	a method or standard of judging	comes from the Greek word *kriterion*

Jumble the papers and challenge a partner to match them correctly.

5. In a group, create a set of rules for making these endings plural: **-on, -um, -is, -us,** and **-a.** Post the rules in your Personal Dictionary, where you can refer to them when needed.

Scroll Back

Edit and proofread your editorial, paying particular attention to the following checklist:

❏ Have you used a variety of sentence structures?
❏ Have you used ellipses correctly with quotations?
❏ Have you applied the principles of plain language to your writing?
❏ Are all words spelled correctly, especially those with Greek or Latin endings?

Unit (16) Résumé and Covering Letter

What are a résumé and covering letter?

Two of the most important forms of persuasive writing are the résumé and the covering letter, because these are the tools people use when applying for jobs. A résumé is a summary of a person's education, work experience, and accomplishments. A covering letter highlights key information in the résumé that is particularly relevant to a specific job.

March 3, 1998

Ms. Josephine Lu
Manager, Prophecy Flower Shop
Eastview Shopping Centre
Red Deer, Alberta
T4N 2W4

Dear Ms. Lu:

I am writing to apply for the job of part-time store helper that was advertised on the bulletin board at Lindsay Thurber High.

My current jobs—delivering papers and babysitting—both require discipline and responsibility, as well as an ability to work well with other people. I also enjoy working with plants. My supervisor at Belview Strawberry Farm taught me a lot about how to care for the plants; I found this work hard but rewarding. And as a Girl Guide and Pathfinder I have always enjoyed taking part in nature projects (one of these gave me practice in classifying plants and wildflowers). Working in a flower store seems like a great way to build on what I have learned.

I would like the opportunity to meet with you to discuss my qualifications. I could start right away for a few days a week after school or on Saturdays, and I would be interested in taking on more hours once school is out for the summer. I look forward to hearing from you, by telephone, mail, or e-mail.

Sincerely,

Janine Gauthier

Janine Gauthier

At the end of this unit you will

Know

- the features of a résumé and covering letter
- three ways to fix a run-on sentence or a comma splice
- some principles of good design
- the proper use of euphemisms in writing
- when to use **c** or **s** in a word

Be Able To

- write your own résumé and covering letter
- recognize run-ons and comma splices in your own writing
- use white space, alignment, headings, and fonts to improve your presentation

---

JANINE T. GAUTHIER

42 Holt Avenue
Red Deer, Alberta T4N 3N2
Telephone: (403) 343-9646 E-mail: jgauth@istar.ca

Education
Sept. 1997–present

Lindsay Thurber Comprehensive High School, Red Deer, Alberta
Currently in Grade 9 French Immersion.

Work Experience
July 1997–present

Newspaper carrier, *The Red Deer Advocate*
Responsible for delivery of a daily paper six days a week to 58 subscribers, and for collecting payments once a month.

June–July 1996, 1997

Strawberry picker, Belview Farms
Worked on a berry farm, picking strawberries and helping to maintain the fields. Advised new workers on field upkeep.

March 1996–present

Babysitter, Ms. Rachel Jardin, Red Deer
Care for two small children, ages three and five, on an occasional basis. Responsible for preparing simple meals and doing light housecleaning.

Interests and Accomplishments
- Member of Pathfinders, a girls' outdoor and adventure group; previously member of Girl Guides (1995–1997)
- St. John Ambulance Babysitting Course (September–October 1993)
- Student of karate at Four Winds School of Self-Defence (1996–present)

References supplied upon request.

147

Checkpoint: Résumé and Covering Letter

Discuss how these characteristics of résumés and covering letters apply to the models. Later, you can use the list to help you revise your own work.

- ✓ The first paragraph of a covering letter usually identifies the position being applied for.

- ✓ The second paragraph highlights skills or experiences relating to the position; the final paragraph requests an interview or other follow-up.

- ✓ Résumés should be brief and to the point; most information is given in point form.

- ✓ Include your name, address, and phone number; education; work experience; and interests and accomplishments.

- ✓ End with a list of references, or a statement that they will be provided upon request.

Writing

1. In your notebook write the headings EDUCATION, WORK EXPERIENCE, INTERESTS, and ACCOMPLISHMENTS. Then list information about yourself below each heading. Arrange the information under each heading in order from most to least recent.

2. Follow the format of the model résumé to create your own. If possible, use a computer.

3. Look through your local newspaper and find a part-time job suitable for a teenager. Cut it out and paste it on a separate sheet of paper; then write a covering letter applying for the job. Be sure to highlight skills and experiences that relate to the job.

4. Refer to the Checkpoint and revise your résumé and covering letter until you are satisfied with their focus, content, and organization.

GRAMMAR

A **run-on sentence** is two or more sentences written as one. A **comma splice** is a type of run-on sentence in which two sentences are joined by a comma.

Know

- three ways to fix a run-on sentence or comma splice

Avoid run-ons such as the following:

Run-On Error: My supervisor at Belview Strawberry Farm taught me a lot about how to care for the plants I found this work hard but rewarding.

Comma Splice Error: My supervisor at Belview Strawberry Farm taught me a lot about how to care for the plants, I found this work hard but rewarding.

Be Able To

- recognize run-ons and comma splices in your own writing

There are three ways to correct run-on sentences:

- Write the run-on sentence as two (or more) separate sentences, using correct punctuation.
- Join the sentences with a semicolon.
- Join the sentences with a conjunction.

1. Which of the three methods do you think works best for the sentences above? Why?

2. Identify the errors in the following sentences and rewrite the sentences correctly.

   a) Janine applied for the job at the flower shop on Tuesday on Thursday she was called for an interview.
   b) Ms. Lu explained the duties Janine would have to perform, Janine listened intently.
   c) Ms. Lu was interested in Janine's work at Belview Strawberry Farm, she asked Janine what she liked most about it.

3. Read the last two or three pieces you have written and see if you can find any run-on sentences and comma splices. If so, copy one of each in your notebook. Rewrite the sentence, correcting the error.

Unit **16**   Résumé and Covering Letter

MECHANICS

The design of a document is important in all forms of writing, but especially in résumés and other forms of business writing.

> Use white space, alignment, headings, and fonts to make your writing easier to read.

- Too many words on a page can make it difficult to read the text. Find ways to condense information and to provide **white space** to make your document attractive and inviting.
- **Align** the text so that important or related information stands out. Placing related information in a line, at the same distance from the left margin, gives the reader a visual clue about the organization of the writing. It also creates white space.

Techno Tip
Many word-processing programs include a "bullet" feature that automatically aligns information and inserts a bullet (•) at the beginning of each line.

- **Headings** help a reader locate specific information at a glance. Using boldface is a good way to make your headings stand out. You may also want to use a bigger typeface or underlining.
- Different **character fonts**, or typefaces, can add interest to a document. However, too many fonts—and fonts that are very intricate—can make a document difficult to read.

1. Look back at the model résumé, and explain how the author has used white space, alignment, headings, and fonts to make information easier to find.

2. Look at your résumé. How could you change the format to make the résumé more reader-friendly?

3. Choose a font from your classroom computer that you think is suitable for each of the following forms of writing. Give reasons for your choices.

   a) an invitation to a child's party
   b) a newspaper advertisement announcing a "midnight madness" sale
   c) a museum brochure describing an exhibition of 18th century paintings

USAGE & STYLE

> A **euphemism** is a pleasant way of expressing something that is unpleasant.

Not every job is glamorous. When used carefully, euphemisms can help to make your experience and qualifications sound as impressive as possible. Read the job experience listed below and note the euphemisms (in italics) used to make them sound more pleasant.

Job Experience:
Labourer at a provincial park: mowing grass, raking the paths, picking up litter, and cleaning the park's pit toilets.

Résumé Description:
Park Support Services Worker
I was responsible for *maintaining* various facilities within the park. Besides *grooming* the grounds and nature trails, I monitored and disposed of *environmental hazards*, and was in charge of *sanitation* at the park's *rest areas*.

However, remember that there's a difference between a euphemism and a falsehood. No employer will hire an applicant who has lied about his or her work and personal history. Nor will anyone be impressed by words that are impossible to understand.

1. Using appropriate euphemisms, create a suitable job title and rewrite the duties associated with the following jobs.

   a) Riswan works weekends as a busboy at a local restaurant. Besides clearing tables and cleaning up spills, he often washes dishes in the kitchen.

   b) Allison sells novelty items door-to-door in her neighbourhood. The items appear in bimonthly and seasonal catalogues, and she places orders for her customers and delivers them when they arrive.

2. Look at your own résumé and decide if there are details that should be replaced with euphemisms to make them sound more appealing.

Unit 16   **Résumé and Covering Letter**

SPELLING

Know

Did you practise your spelling today, or do you not need practice? **C** or **s**—there are only twelve words where you have to make this choice. In this unit, you have a chance to practise (practice?) these words.

Words to Watch For

Some of these words have been taken from the letter and résumé at the beginning of the unit. Others have been added to represent words you may need to learn to spell.

advice	defence	offence	practice	prophecy
advise	defense	offense	practise	prophesy

1. If a **licence** is a permit to drive, what does **license** mean? Look up the word in a dictionary, then use it in a sentence.

Strategy

When you write you may find that you can't think of a word, or you know the word but aren't sure of its spelling. Don't interrupt your writing. Write the letters you do know in the word. After you've finished your draft, go back and complete the spelling of the word, using a reference if necessary.

2. Read these sentences. Which of the two words in boldface is a noun, and which is a verb?

   a) Etienne's father gave him this **advice** about his interview: "Arrive on time."

   b) If you want, I can **advise** you about clothes to wear to the interview.

3. Reread the first sentence of this spelling unit. Based on how the words *practise* and *practice* are used, write two new sentences that show the meaning of each word.

4. With *advise* and *advice,* one spelling is used for the verb and the other for the noun. The *defence/defense* and *offence/offense* pairs are examples of a different spelling issue. With a partner, discuss why there are two spellings of each word. You might need to check one or more dictionaries to learn the answer.

5. You're now familiar with all words that can be spelled with either a **c** or **s.** Write a short note—a mnemonic, a poem, lines of text—that would help someone learn at least two of these spellings.

Scroll Back

Edit and proofread your résumé and covering letter, paying particular attention to the following checklist:

❏ Have you avoided run-ons and comma splices?
❏ Have you used white space, alignment, headings, and fonts appropriately?

Present It!

Edit your résumé and covering letter very carefully for possible errors. First impressions are very important, and errors will suggest to an employer that you have not taken care with your application. Have someone else edit your work, too, before making a final copy.

Unit 16 Résumé and Covering Letter

Word List

155

Word List

Index